Promote God's Kingdom!

In Christ.

Rom 1:16

POINT OF DECISION

God's Provision vs Man's Solution

Based on the Biblical account of Ruth

by Robert D. Kee

ISBN: 1544709919
ISBN 13: 9781544709918
Library of Congress Control Number: 2017910774
CreateSpace Independent Publishing Platform
North Charleston, South Carolina

INDEX

DEDICATION

Words escape me to manifest the immensity of emotions and gratitude I have for the eternal and ultimate power, grace, mercy and love that my Heavenly Father has so graciously poured out on me through His Son Jesus Christ. If I were to pass from this life today I have experienced more blessings than I deserve.

The inspiration that spurs me on and keeps me believing that maybe, just maybe, I can make a difference in the world is fueled by those who love me most, my family.

To my wife, Belinda: Your love and encouragement are what continually give me hope even in the midst of self-doubt. Thank you for believing in me and inspiring me to believe in myself. I love you Sweetheart!

To my son, Robert: Your confidence in my ability and your desire to have something to pass down to future generations was a driving factor for me to finish this work. Thank you for your steadfast confidence. I love you Son!

To my daughter, Laurén: Your belief in me and childlike faith was never more clear than when you helped copy and organize all of the transcripts to prepare them for editing. Your smile and hugs kept me going. Thank you Sweetgirl, I love you!

Thank you to my wonderful daughter inlaw, and my precious grandchildren for your constant love and encouragement. And thanks to my mother, father, sister and her family for the constant prayers over the years.

A big hug and thanks to all of my friends and family who have continually and patiently redirected me back to this project to insure it's completion. You are all such a blessing. Without your persistence you would not be reading this right now.

An additional thanks to the prayers and patience of the congregations of Harvest Christian Center of Corning, CA and Generations United of Lompoc, CA.

~ CONTACT INFO ~
Requests for speaking engagements can be emailed to:
Rob@RobKeeSolutions.com

ACKNOWLEDGEMENTS

Transcription: Marie Hoffman
Editors: Rachel Alexander, Belinda Kee, Robert S. Kee, Lori Kee, Lauren Kee, Nick Alexander, Gib Hullinger
Biblical Counsel: Nick Alexander, Robert S. Kee, Ed Goble, Sandy Querin
Resources:
King James Version Bible
Halley's Bible Handbook 25th Edition
Merriam Webster's Dictionary
Oxford American Dictionary
Strong's Concordance

DESPERATE DESIRE

As you begin to turn the pages through this journey I would first like to ask you a question.

How desperate are you to find and know God?

I mean really, really know Him? At times in your spiritual pursuit you seemed to be very willing to do "certain things" for God and even go "certain places" for Him. At the peaks of your spiritual experience, you have said that you were "completely" sold out for Him, but closer examination reveals that there are still several areas of your life that are alien to God's presence because you have never allowed Him to fully dwell there and perform His work.

Isn't God big enough to handle even the quarantined areas of your life? My challenge to you is to let Him in, give Him permission to wreck your preconceptions of your "normal" and see what happens.

So how desperate are you? Before you answer take a moment to join a young man on his journey as he comes face to face with the reality of desperation.

This young man sincerely believed he was desperate to find God. He searched high and low to no avail. Finally someone told him that if he truly wanted the key to finding God he would have to go talk to the old wise man that lived deep in the forest next to the river.

The young man fought weather, elements and wild animals on his journey and finally came to the wise man's home. The wise man saw the young man coming and inquired of his purpose for visiting him.

The young man went on to tell the wise man of his desperate quest to find God and that he was told the wise man could help him. The old wise man rested back in his chair looking up at the sky and asked, "So you want to find God?" The young man replied, "Yes".

At this the wise man raised up in his chair leaning forward now looking at the young man and asked the question again, "So you really want to find God?" Again the young man replied, "Yes!"

The wise man then standing to his feet and looking the young man square in the eye restated his question and presented it with a deep passion, "How badly do you want to find God?" The young man responded with a sense of frustrated desperation and said, "I want to find God more than anything that is within me. Nothing matters to me more than this quest!"

With this the old wise man motioned for the young man to follow him and together they walked toward the river that flowed in front of the wise man's house.

Once they arrived at the bank of the river, the wise man walked the young man out to a ledge that dropped him into the water just below his chin line. The wise man still perched on the ledge, knelt down to speak to the young man.

The wise man asked, "Are you ready, my son?" The young man, shivering from the icy water, yet excited to finally acquire the key to finding God, immediately replied, "Yes, I am ready!" The old man grabbed the young man by his head and shoved him under the ice-cold water, holding him under for a few brief seconds.

As the old man pulled the young man's head above the water the young man gasped for air and cried out, "What are you trying to do? Are you trying to kill me?" The words had no more left the young man's lips when the old man grabbed his head and shoved him down for a second time, this time holding him under for almost a full minute.

The young man resurfaced, gasping for air, choking on the water and with an angry tone began to shout at the old man, "I'm going to drown! I am helpless out here in this deep water. You are going to kill me!"

Again the words had not fully escaped his lips and the wise man took him down for a third time. This time holding him down until the fight had almost completely left the young man. The old man then pulled him up out of the water just in time.

The young man, already turning purple, desperately gasping for air while spitting up water, cried out to the old man, "Please, spare my life!" The wise man quietly helped him up and went to sit on the bank of the river. The young man finding the strength to crawl over by the wise teacher collapsed on the ground in front of him as he continued to gasp for each breath.

Several minutes passed when the wise man broke the silence by asking the young man, "What was it that you desired more than anything during those last few moments under the water? What was it that you would have given anything to get? At that moment, what was it that was more valuable than anything you could ever be offered?"

The young man responded without hesitation, "AIR! I would have given anything, even my soul, for one more breath!"

The wise old man smiled as he looked squarely into the young man's face and said, "You have now acquired the key you so longed for. When your desire to find God becomes so desperate that you would do anything, go anywhere, and give even your own soul in this pursuit, then, and only then you will find Him. Even better, He will find you!" As the young man left the old wise man that day, he was rejoicing and praising God. He realized that nothing in his life was worth anything without God!

"At that moment, what was it that was more valuable than anything you could ever be offered?"

How desperate are we to find God and to know Him? Taking the layers of our pseudo Christianity away, would we find a deep desperate desire to find God, or would we find that our true passion lies elsewhere?

My prayer is that this brief writing will invoke a desperate desire, a burning unquenchable passion to pursue God and know Him intimately for yourself. Remember He is already here waiting for you. He pursued you when you had no desire to pursue Him. He has already paid the price and has reconciled you back to Himself.

Will you inquire? Will you pursue? Will you search? Will you find? The choice is yours. Welcome to the journey of one who did, a young Moabite widow named Ruth.

"And ye shall seek me, and find me, when ye shall search for me with all your heart." Jeremiah 29:13 (KJV)

INTRODUCTION
EMBRACING THE BOUNDARIES

This writing is not meant to be an exhaustive study, but rather a study companion to the Book of Ruth. I hope you underline, highlight and scribble your personal thoughts in the margins. My prayer is that you will be able to go back to your journal entries throughout the years and find fresh insight that you may someday pass along to your children.

Some of the thoughts or ideas projected are not word for word from the characters or text of the original story and may reflect my personal opinions on how certain situations may have played out in these types of scenarios.

There is no intention to change the Word of God or twist the meaning of any passage. I am only attempting to convey my personal convictions as I have seen them through my study of this wonderful story of redemption.

Today we begin a journey that will challenge your perspective of decision making and help you understand the far reaching effects of each choice you make before you make it. The ultimate goal is to reveal the great lengths God has gone in order to reconcile you back to Himself. It is my prayer that a desperate desire to know Him will empower you to annihilate your selfish-will and walk in His Spirit.

In the process of freeing you by the sacrifice of His Son, Jesus Christ, from everything that separates you from Himself, God has given us the privilege to also invest in this freedom by giving us the power to release.

For you to experience this freedom you must be willing to let go of everything, and make Him your source of life as well as your only focus of passion. Like the young man, your hunger for God must be desperate and supersede even your desire to breathe.

Do you want God as much as you need air? Do you really mean it? Do you really want to depend on God with the same desperation that you long for your next breath, knowing that without it death is imminent? Do you really want God's direction for your life? Do you really want to hear His voice?

You may hesitate because you know when you do hear His voice, it will require something. God might require something of you that you're not ready to let go of, not ready to release!

We think of obedience as some huge disciplinary act, but only because discipline requires living within established boundaries. The boundaries set by God will guarantee a promise of hope, a hope that the world longs for, but without God they can never attain.

As someone once said, "Today is the first day of the rest of your life." So let's begin a journey today that will provoke in you a celebration of these boundaries embracing them as a safeguard to keep you on the right path, fully equipping you to make good decisions, breaking generational cycles to produce a legacy you can be proud of.

Choose to live within His boundaries of freedom. Stand on God's promises and allow Him to direct your path, following His lead every step of the way.

"…let's begin a journey that will provoke in you a celebration of these boundaries, to embrace them as a safeguard to keep you on the right path, fully equipping you to make good decisions, breaking generational cycles to produce a legacy you can be proud of."

CHAPTER 1
THE POWER TO RELEASE

Ruth 1:1-2

Now it came to pass in the days when the judges ruled, that there was a famine in the land. And a certain man of Beth–lehem–judah went to sojourn in the country of Moab, he, and his wife, and his two sons. And the name of the man was Elimelech, and the name of his wife Naomi, and the name of his two sons Mahlon and Chilion, Ephrathites of Beth–lehem–judah. And they came into the country of Moab, and continued there.

This story begins with the wide stroke of a very bleak brush. Famine was ravaging the land of Bethlehem-Judah. The period of the Judges seems to have been coming to an end. Whether it was related to a growing moral decadence in the land or just an act of nature, it is unknown, but for whatever reason, a famine had swept across what was once known as "The Land of Bread" apparently leaving families hungry, homeless and destitute. There was not enough food to go around and only the rich were afforded the luxury of owning property and what was left of the crops.

One of the families affected by this tragedy was that of Elimelech. Elimelech was married to Naomi and together they had two sons, Mahlon and Chilion. Let's take a closer look at Elimelech for insight on what provoked the initiation of this journey. He and his family were from the land of Judah. Drought and famine plagued the territory. Food was scarce, to say the least, and to feed a family was next to impossible. Looking around Elimelech weighed out the options and made the difficult decision to move his family from Judah to Moab where the famine didn't seem to have had the same affect on the land and food was more readily available.

At first glance, Elimelech's decision seems like one a responsible husband and father would make; just a regular guy trying to take care of his family, making sure they have food on the table. But on closer examination this one simple act of self-preservation was actually a pivotal decision that could have detrimentally changed the course of their family history forever.

Ruth 1:3-5

And Elimelech Naomi's husband died; and she was left, and her two sons. And they took them wives of the women of Moab; the name of the one was Orpah, and the name of the other Ruth: and they dwelled there about ten years. And Mahlon and Chilion died also both of them; and the woman was left of her two sons and her husband.

Ok wait, we aren't even a quarter of the way into the first chapter when we find Elimelech and his two sons dead leaving behind three widows? Scripture provides no explanation as to why these men died, but nevertheless they are dead and Naomi is makes the difficult decision to leave her two daughters in-law and returning to her homeland of Judah. As she does the one daughter in-law, Orpah, sorrowfully chooses to stay in Moab while the other, Ruth, decides to abandon everything she has called home and accompany her mother-in-law on her journey. Years earlier Elimelech made a critical life decision that set his family up for utter extinction. Now Naomi made the decision to return home, and because of that Ruth made her own critical life decision. A decision which will chart the course of her life from this point on ultimately leading her to a destination she could have never imagined.

Ruth 1:6-18

Then she (Naomi) arose with her daughters in law, that she might return from the country of Moab: for she had heard in the country of Moab how that the Lord had visited his people in giving them bread. Wherefore she went forth out of the place where she was, and her two daughters in law with her; and they went on the way to return unto the land of Judah. And Naomi said unto her two daughters in law, Go, return each to her mother's house: the Lord deal kindly with you, as ye have dealt with the dead, and with me. The Lord grant you that ye may find rest, each of you in the house of her husband. Then she kissed them; and they lifted up their voice, and wept. And they said unto her, Surely we will return with thee unto thy people. And Naomi said, Turn again, my daughters: why will ye go with me? are there yet any more sons in my womb, that they may be your husbands? Turn again, my daughters, go your way; for I am too old to have an husband. If I should say, I have hope, if I should have an husband also to night, and should also bear sons; Would ye tarry for them till they were grown? would ye stay for them from having husbands? nay, my daughters; for it grieveth me much for your sakes that the hand of the Lord is gone out against me. And they lifted up their voice, and wept again: and Orpah kissed her mother-in-law; but Ruth clave unto her. And she said, Behold, thy sister in law is gone back unto her people, and unto her gods: return thou after thy sister in law. And Ruth said, Entreat me not to leave thee, or to return from following after thee: for whither thou goest, I will go; and where thou lodgest, I will lodge: thy people shall be my people, and thy God my God: Where thou diest, will I die, and there will I be buried: the Lord do so to me, and more also, if ought but death part thee and me. When she saw that she was stedfastly minded to go with her, then she left speaking unto her.

Our individual decisions really do affect others. The often repeated mantra, "It's my decision, it doesn't affect anyone else…", is a lie and one of satan's most tactical weapons.

I was twenty-one years old and about to become a father with my beautiful bride. We were so excited and couldn't wait for the special day to come. I worked on a petroleum pipeline crew as a heavy equipment operator and traveled a lot, which meant I was continuously away from home. I knew I would need to be closer and more available so we could attend all of our necessary classes to get ready for the birth of our baby and I wanted to be home each night in case my wife went into labor.

I felt confident that this was God's leading and a good decision for my growing family. So I spoke to my boss about the situation and asked to be placed on a different crew for a while so I could be there for my wife. Due to the fact I was on a specialty crew, the only one in the company that could perform some of the hazardous procedures the job often required, he was obviously unimpressed. Naturally he began sharing his stories of how he was out of town on a pipeline job when his baby was born and everything went fine, his wife didn't even need him there to have the baby.

I remained unmoved, until he started appealing to my "provider-exceller" instinct. It was my desire to provide for my family and excelling in the company would give me a better chance at making more money and obtaining more security in the pipeline industry. Yep, you guessed it. The next words out of his mouth were, "How about I give you a promotion and a raise?" Ba'am, just like that he had me. I reasoned that it must be God's will for me to take it since it was such a large raise and a great opportunity. Besides, he told me that we wouldn't be on the road again for at least a few months. How could I turn him down, it was everything I was hoping for! I had already forgotten that just moments ago I was convinced God had lead this decision.

Well wouldn't you know it. Oh yes I got the raise and the promotion, but by the next week my crew was contracted out to a project that would keep me on the road and away from home for the next four months. This decision would affect the security of my young wife and maybe even keep me from being there for the birth of the baby who would be my son. In one brief moment I had made the decision to leave the Land of God's Provision and launch out into the land of my solution.

One single act, just one simple decision, can not only change your life, but many generations to follow. What choices are you making that are going to chart the course of your life and the lives of those you love? Where are the effects of those decisions leading you? Take a moment to reflect on these questions and more than likely you'll face some difficult truths in your own life. But if you face them now you'll be able to make the necessary adjustments to get back on course.

Have you suffered harsh consequences from decisions made by others? Have you been victimized by those you trusted? Now what about you? Have you ever victimized anyone by your poor choices or made the innocent suffer the consequences of your decisions?

It's time for change! You've been given the Power to Release so start exercising it. Start releasing the hurt and pain both that you have suffered and that which you are responsible for. Jesus said that we must forgive if we want to be forgiven (Matthew 6:9). Stop being overcome with evil, and start overcoming evil with good! (Romans 12:21)

"It's time for change! You've been given the Power to Release…"

Enforce the power to release and begin reversing the inevitable outcome of poor choices. Make the decision to follow

Christ Jesus today and allow Him to re-chart the course of your family's destiny.

Please accept my challenge to you. Explore the caverns of your heart and cry out to God with the absolute desperation that is required to find Him. A desperation to do anything, go anywhere, and give even your own soul in this pursuit. Then be silent and wait, and He will find you.

CHAPTER 2
THE GOD DECISION

E limelech thought he was making a 'good' decision, but the problem was this, it wasn't a 'God' decision. There is no record of Elimelech ever taking the time to inquire of God. Only that "he chose" to take his family to the land of Moab. Let's take a quick look at the land of Moab. Who were the Moabites and what did they stand for? Have I ever made 'good' decisions that weren't 'God' decisions?

A 'good' decision is one that is not morally wrong, but is not necessarily God's plan. It is birthed out of impulse and self-preservation of your needs, wants and desires being the central focus and benefactor. A 'God' decision is one that has been birthed out of time spent with the Father. This decision is selfless and reveals God's specific direction for you and your family and ultimately brings glory to Jesus!

"A 'God' decision is one that has been birthed out of time spent with the Father."

There are two keys that we have already been given to help us make more 'God' decisions and spend less time on the 'good' ones.

First, our desire for God's direction must be desperate, just like our need for air. So much so that we seek and inquire of Him regardless of personal cost. James tells us that if we desire wisdom we need to ask for it and God will freely give it to us if our intentions are pure (James 1:5).

Secondly, we must exercise our newfound Power to Release. Paul tells us that we are to take our vain imaginations captive (2 Corinthians 10:3-7). We must release the familiar, the things seen with our natural eye, submitting to Christ all of our insecurities and even those things with which we have grown secure. Releasing all we have acquired so we may grasp all He has offered.

Moab was a foreign land, a cursed land (Deut 23:6), a land that was outside of the promise of God for His children, Israel. How many times have we, on our own, made a decision to leave the land of promise? Moabite territory was a land birthed out of incest. If you remember the story Moab's father was also his grandfather. Weird right? See (Genesis 12-19).

Lot was Abraham's nephew. When Abraham left his hometown of Ur and embarked on his journey to seek the city that God had built for him, his nephew Lot, brought his family along. It is unclear whether Abraham invited Lot to come or Lot invited himself. Genesis chapter 12 says that only Abraham was given the word by God to leave his homeland, and then says that "Abraham departed,... and Lot went with him."

So the two families departed Ur and traveled together. A point to be made here is that if God gave a Word to YOU, then you'd better make sure you are only traveling with those that He has directed you to travel with or the mission could be compromised. Was Abraham's decision to allow Lot to come with him a good decision or a God decision?

"...if God gave a Word to YOU, then you'd better make sure you are only traveling with those that He has directed you to travel with or the mission could be compromised."

Nevertheless, the Bible tells us that Abraham and Lot's herds and flocks became so large that their servants began to fight among themselves, each side trying to insure that there was enough open land for each family's livestock to graze. Abraham saw what was going on and realized that the land they were traveling through was too small for both families and their flocks to co-habitate. He then suggested to Lot that they split up and go separate ways to prevent further confrontations.

Abraham was Lot's elder uncle, and although there is no record of this it would seem that out of respect Lot should have been the one to suggest that he put some space between their families so as not to create an issue. Lot was the leader of those that were under his care, he should have told his servants to back off, since they were technically the guests on the journey, and respect the people they were traveling with. Sadly this did not appear to be the case. This apparent lack of ability to make a responsible decision would lead to his eventual demise and bring God's judgment upon an entire nation.

Abraham must have recognized this character flaw in his nephew and knew if he said anything it may have become a bigger problem. With that in mind Abraham offered Lot to make the fist choice. Abraham would then go in the opposite direction to avoid conflict. Lot looks around and sees a dry, barren land, nothing attractive or seducing at all. "No reason to go there", he must have thought to himself. But as he continues to gaze on the landscape he sees a land of green pastures and apparent prosperity. "That's it! That's the direction I'll go!" Was Lot's decision a good decision or a God decision? What do you think?

I could be way off on this, but it sure looks like another decision motivated by circumstance. "I am going to send old Uncle Abe, who is much older than I am, into the middle of nowhere with his family while I go to set up my home in a land of prosperity." What was Lot thinking? Oh wait, it's pretty apparent that he was thinking about himself! So we find Lot and his family setting up home in their new town. Sodom and Gomorrah, a place of moral decadence, a place where there was no fear of the Almighty God whatsoever, a place where sin surged and sexual immorality reigned. A place so dark you could feel the weight of its presence stealing each breathe from you. Yep, this was the place Lot chose for his family to call home. The very place where he, his wife and two daughters would eventually succumb to the passions of society.

Lot's focus seemed to be wrong to begin with, but now it wasn't even in the same hemisphere. How many times have you had the wrong motive? Or how many times have you been on a journey that in the beginning seemed clear as to its intended purpose, but the way gets tiresome and long, and the landscape seems to hold nothing but a destiny of dry barrenness. If you're not careful, you will end up being driven by circumstance and choosing our own way. It may look good at first, but it eventually numbs your senses to the Spirit of God and derails His original direction for your life.

"If we're not careful, we end up being driven by circumstance and choosing our own way."

That's exactly what happened to Lot. He became so desensitized to God's Spirit that he wouldn't even obey when He sent angels to his door to save him from the judgment that was coming upon the city. Think about it for a moment, just prior to this Abraham had pleaded with the Lord to save his nephew and his family even though Lot's treatment of his uncle was less than honorable. In God's mercy, because He loved Abraham, He sends angels to Lot's house telling him to "GET OUT!" so his family could be saved from the wrath that was coming.

Lot should have grabbed his family and left town immediately! Then he should have spent the rest of his life thanking God for His mercy in spite of his poor decision to become a part of such an evil community. But no, how does Lot respond to the angelic messengers? Something like this, "Hey guys, come on in and let's talk about this for a while. Surely we can work something out." He tried reasoning with them. REASONING WITH THEM? Are you kidding me?

Stupid, stupid, stupid! Why didn't he just obey? Why? Because his heart had been seared. He had allowed society to affect him rather than him affecting society. As the angels tried to speak to Lot a hostile group of local men, whom Lot referred to as 'brothers', began to break down the door of his home demanding that he send the angels out so they could rape them. What? Seriously? Good job Lot, you really know how to pick your neighbors.

It would seem obvious that even righteous Lot was susceptible to the influence of society. In 2 Peter 2:6-8, we are told that Lot was considered by God to be a righteous man, the he was actually grieved by the wickedness he saw around him. I believe this serves as a prime example of how we as Christians can be burdened by the evil we see around us, but not be effective in standing against it. He had absolutely no influence on the fellow residents he called 'brothers'.

The true Christian are called to stand for righteousness in the midst of anything that is unacceptable and contradictory to God's message of grace. We are to show the uncompromising love of God. Not condoning, accepting or even tolerating sinful behavior, but loving the individual. This is true with any behavior that opposes the Holiness of God.

As Christians we must always remember that God created us all in His image and that He sent His Son to save us from our sinful, fallen state and reconcile us back to Himself. Today it seems that we not only take 'no stand' against sin, we willfully with open eyes, accept a wide array of sin under the guise of the new "Tolerance" standard, once again succumbing to the passions of society and political correctness.

"...we willfully, with open eyes, accept a wide array of sin under the guise of the new "Tolerance" standard..."

We as the Church, the Body of Christ, have grown calloused to the voice of God and the Holiness He requires. Regardless of what we are being told by those who are trying to erase our Godly heritage, we as a nation were founded on Jesus Christ and the God of the Christian Bible for the sole purpose of spreading the Gospel message (See the Mayflower Compact). Over the past few decades, we have made decisions that have gradually turned the heart of our country away from the principles on which we were founded. We have made decisions to accept those things that oppose God and have hardened our hearts to the voice of the Holy Spirit. We no longer acknowledge right from wrong.

Sin becomes predominant in our lives when Christ is no longer preeminent! We have allowed ourselves to compromise God's Word and twist it into an unnatural state of relevance that will tolerate the sin that the world embraces. We have sold our souls to satan, and have lost site of the standard of Holiness He demands. Yes, we have followed the way of Lot and become ineffective in our witness for Christ.

"Sin becomes predominant in our lives when Christ is no longer preeminent!"

After being turned away and refused access to the angels, this angry mob incites a riot and threatens Lot and his family with bodily harm, worse that that which they planned for the two angelic beings, unless they yield to their sexually perverted demands. All this and yet still Lot lingers. The angels, moved by the Lord's mercy, grabbed Lot and his family by the hands and lead, or more accurately dragged them out of the city. It's almost like the family really didn't want to go. Oh that's right, it's because they didn't!

The angels give Lot specific instruction as to where they are to go for protection. But Lot does it again! Yep, being unimpressed by the angelic advice, he begins to negotiate. It may have sounded something like this, "Ok angels I get why you're doing this, but realistically the place you're sending us to is in the middle of nowhere. Can't you send us into a better city? My wife really enjoyed the malls, the shopping and her social circles back in Sodom. I mean, come on, don't you think it's going to be hard enough for her to make the already difficult changes just being away from home? Well, what do you think? Hey look, there's another city. It looks a little more lively, how about that one?" Frustrated, the angel responds, "GO! Just go!" I can only imagine, angels or not, they must have been glad when their interaction with Lot was over.

Ungodly compromise never solves anything. Lot thought he could solve the obvious irritation of his wife by supplying an alternate route than the one chosen for them by God. As usual that didn't help anything. His wife still couldn't pull herself away from the passions of her past and chose to look back on Sodom with a longing to return. In doing so, her life ended as she immediately turned into a pillar of salt, its hardness only surpassed by that of her heart. Lot and his two daughters continued the journey and after a a series of events, they were ostracized from the town they chose to escape to retreating to the wilderness. Lot and his two daughters found themselves in a place of hopelessness dwelling in a cave, alone. But one bad decision just seems to lead to another with this guy and his family.

Rather than turning their hearts back to God for direction, Lot's daughters followed their father's example, they let circumstance dictate their decision. They must have been discussing their bleak future as they sat just outside the entrance of the cave and began to fear the thought of being childless since it appeared there was no one for them to marry. In this lack of belief for God to sustain them, they devised a plan of self-preservation which would take future generations into a deep pit of moral perversion and affect their family forever. Was this decision to insure self-preservation a good decision or a God decision?

They finalized their plan by getting their father, Lot, drunk. After he was unaware of what was going on, both of them took their turns having sex with their father and conceived his children. In summary, Lot who was the father to his daughters became the father to his grandsons. This entire scene was a product of Lot's seared heart provoked by his decision not to inquire of the Lord for direction years earlier when his uncle Abraham gave him the opportunity to choose which way to go. Or possibly even earlier still, whether or not he should have ever left his home town Ur in the first place. Only God truly knows.

Lot, who was the husband and father of his family, failed in his duties to his wife and daughters because he allowed himself to be driven by the highest bidder for self-gratification. Even as one the New Testament reveals to be a righteous man, Lot demonstrates to us the subtle ways we can lose sight of the battle and our responsibility to protect those God has entrusted to us. It's definitely not a foreign concept to humanity. Take a minute to read about King David and his lust for a woman that was so strong it drove him to commit adultery with her then have her husband killed in order to hide his own sin (See 2 Samuel 11).

So Lot named his grandson, which was also his son, Moab. This child, birthed out of the immoral union between a father and daughter, became the father of the Moabites. A nation birthed out of incest, selfish lusts and fear. This is where we find Elimelech and his family.

Have you made good decisions that weren't God decisions? Take a moment and write one down. Now go to the Father, repent of your decision and your lack of prayer that led you to that place. Ask Him to show you how to rectify the situation and then pray healing for all of the individuals affected by your choice. We will only be realigned with God when we yield ourselves in obedience to His Holy Word, and obey the Holy Spirit's leading. "We need to stop settling for the 'good' and hold out for the 'God'!"

It is absolutely necessary to seek God before making decisions in our lives. Many times we think that just because something seems like a good idea that it must be a God idea. Not so. We will continue on our journey with Elimelech and his family as we watch their story unfold.

"We need to stop settling for the 'good' and hold out for the 'God'!"

CHAPTER 3

PREPARING FOR REDEMPTION

B efore continuing we must finish painting the true bleakness of this picture in order to have every opportunity to grasp an understanding of how desperate Elimelech's situation truly was. Only when we are real about the depravity of our circumstances, can we honestly see God at work in the midst of our situation. The bleaker the picture, the more intense the power of God's redemption, and the more real it becomes to us on an intimate level of relationship.

> **"Only when we are real with the depravity of our circumstances can we honestly see God at work in the midst of our situation."**

Accountability is a byword that eases our conscience, but is thwarted at the smallest sign of being held responsible for questionable behaviors. Some rarely ever know the fruit of their destructive actions. The moment they begin to feel the painful effects of their bad decisions some well-intentioned person runs in to buffer the effect. They're offered excuses for justification, "It's all right, God knows, nobody's perfect." Or the old, "Oh well, live and learn." The offending person embraces these as reality and becomes oblivious to the impact of their decision, the destruction left in its wake.

It's not that we shouldn't come alongside of those who have hurt themselves by their own willful acts of disobedience, we should. But we need to carefully listen to God's voice as to how much comfort we are to provide. If we're not careful, we end up robbing God of glory, and the person of the opportunity to learn from and not repeat their harmful past.

Too much of the time, we get between a wayward child and God's disciplinary hand. As a Father, I love my children enough that there are times I need to implement discipline in order to correct bad behavioral patterns before it gets them into serious trouble. Never get between my discipline and my child. Doing this assumes that you know what's best for 'my' child, it undermines my parental authority and breeds disrespect in my child toward me.

"Be careful not to be found guilty of obstructing the work of God's disciplinary hand."

Be careful not to be found guilty of obstructing the work of God's disciplinary hand. Rest in the fact that He loves the individual more than you ever could and He knows what is best for them. Remember His perspective is not limited, He sees everything from an eternal point of view.

Moab was a land, true to its origin, filled with sexual immorality, murder and perversion. The Moabites were key players in idol worship and infanticide, the practice of murdering babies for the sake of social or personal gain, in this case offering their helpless little lives up as sacrifices to their god Molech. (Read Leviticus 20:1-8 for God's thoughts on Molech and the participants of this practice. Then do some research on the over 57 million babies murdered in the United States via abortion and ask yourself if we're really that much different.)

Maybe this is just a random thought, but shouldn't it have dawned on Elimelech that it wasn't such a good idea, moving his family to a place where its very name represents sin, rebellion, incest and even baby sacrificing? His heart had already become hardened. He was no longer being moved by the voice of God, but rather by the pull of circumstance. Bethlehem-Judah was in the middle of a severe drought and famine, and Elimelech was looking for a way out, he was desperate.

At first glance we might say, "Be easy on the guy, he was just trying to take care of his family." But as an Israelite, truly trying to take care of his family, he would have sought God for direction first. It's easy to judge Elimelech, but if we are honest, we have done the exact same thing. Even as a true Christ-follower if you are not listening, not praying, not reading God's Word, you can fall into a place of hardness and complacency that will take you down a road you would have never normally chose for yourself.

"We should be desperate for only one thing, to know God."

Sadly there is no evidence that alludes to Elimelech ever inquiring or seeking God's face in his decision. We have all been there, haven't we? We've all made decisions without consulting God and we've all paid the price. Elimelech made his decision not realizing the impact that it was going to have on his family for generations to come. We should spend more time asking God for direction before we make a decision, instead of reacting in desperation and asking forgiveness for the wrong choice we made. We should be desperate for only one thing, to know God.

In Elimelech's day if an Israelite were to marry a Moabite, their family name would be removed from the genealogy of Israel for ten generations until the genealogical line was considered purified (Deuteronomy 23:3). Ten generations had to suffer the consequence of one person's decision to walk outside of God's will. Just one!

With this in mind, a good friend made a point that is worth sharing. Some might ask, "Why was it ok for Elimilech's sons to marry Moabite women?" Scripture is very clear about God's feelings on Israel intermarrying with those from idol-worshiping foreign countries and Deuteronomy 7:3-4a tells us why:

> *"You shall not intermarry with them, giving your daughters to their sons or taking their daughters for your sons, for they would turn away your sons from following me, to serve other gods."*

The answer is this, it was not okay for his sons to marry Moabite woman. This was another product of Elimilech's decision. The fact that Ruth, a moabite woman, was accepted by God and used to restore Naomi's inheritance is an example of God's grace and Ruth's humility.

"God resisteth the proud, and giveth grace to the humble."
1 Peter 5:5b

Maybe Elimelech should have thought a little bit more about this before 'diving in' or maybe better said 'jumping out' of God's will and exposing his family to foreign gods in a foreign land. I despise our pious attitudes when we spout off ludicrous statements like, "It's my decision!" Or, "It only affects me, it's no one else's business?"

That popularized attitude in nothing more than a demon that crawled out from under a rock and is whispering in the ear of anyone who will listen and willingly be its mouthpiece. Never again be guilty of believing or perpetuating this lie. Let's be clear. Every decision you make affects you and those around you for generations to come.

How many times have we exposed our families to foreign gods? To greed, lust, incest; to adultery, homosexuality, pornography; to violence, crime, lies, gossip, and deceit; to addictions and cyclic patterns in our families that we continue to foster. Instead of falling at the feet of Jesus and crying out for help, we continue setting our family up to repeat these generational curses.

Maybe this is a good time to pause and ask yourself, "Is this what I am doing?" If so, then what are you going to do to change these destructive behavioral patterns?

"Elimelech…minimized the impact of his influence."

Elimelech did what many of us do when we've made a bad decision, he minimized the impact of his influence. What he didn't realize was that he was living this example in front of his family. His actions shouted, "It's okay to be driven by circumstance". He needed more of the Fear of God which would have put at ease his fear of the circumstance.

No one likes to go hungry, no one wants to see their family go without. Yet the fact remains he was in the Promise Land, he was in Judah. He was in the place where God promised to take care of His people if they would follow His commands. When the circumstances changed, Elimelech forgot the promise of God. "I don't 'see' it God. I don't 'see' Your promise, so it must no longer be true."

Instead of consulting God and building his faith as his father Abraham did time and time again. He must have figured that God couldn't handle this one so he needed to step in and do something. It was time for the infamous "Plan-B".

You know, the same option you grab for when God doesn't meet the need like you told Him he should. "I need to figure out a way to provide for my family since God has obviously let down on the job. I know God said I am a child of promise; I know that God gave me this land; I know He said He's my healer, my deliverer and my provider. But something went wrong, and I guess I need to fix it." So off he goes, walking right out of the will of God, with his wife, kids and whatever was left of their possessions following closely behind.

"We make decisions every day, some of which lead us right out of God's will not even giving it a second thought."

We make decisions every day, some of which lead us right out of God's will not even giving it a second thought and find that things aren't going right, things didn't come together like we had planned. We make decisions in relationships, in our lives, our marriages, our careers and our ministries that lack integrity and then try to justify it as "Well, nobody's perfect." Poor choices in our finances, poor spending habits, increasing our debt load, never counting the cost. We made a conscience choice not to inquire of God beforehand then we cry out, "Oh, God, deliver us!" The products of these decisions keep peering through the curtain of the generations that follow and we wonder why.

Even something as simple as debt. We justify it to ourselves, "It's no big deal; I've got a good job. I get a regular paycheck so I can afford it." If that's your attitude, as it is with many in our nation's capital, then you still don't get it! If you died today, somebody would have to pay your bill. The fact of the matter is, we've been taught as a society that when we create debt we don't have to be responsible for it. From the 'House of God' to the 'White House', as Americans, we are taught financial irresponsibility from birth. We are all guilty. These things affect you, your children and your children's children.

What Elimelech did not realize, is that it was God's intent for them to be a part of the bloodline of Jesus Christ himself. And he almost blew it – totally! If it weren't for the grace of God and the obedience of a young Moabitess named Ruth his family line would have been blotted out and would have never made it into the Messiah's genealogy as recorded in the Gospel according to the book of Matthew chapter 1.

The decisions that you make are not just about you. They are about those who are with you as well as those who will come after you.

"God will always take care of His obligation!"

God will always take care of His obligation! Position yourself to hear His voice by standing on the truth of His Word, focusing your eyes on Him and keeping your end of the covenant, to obey His Word, He will always fulfill His promise.

Elimelech set his family up for failure. As a parent, how many times have you set your children up for failure? We wonder why they don't want to go to school. Could it be that you whined around about all of your childhood memories of hating school and your rebellion toward the teachers and principal?

Your adult children can never hold down a job. Is it because maybe you couldn't hold down a job? Instead of being accountable for your own attitudes and actions, you always blamed that idiot of a boss, your incapable co-workers, or the 'inhumane' conditions you had to work in?

But of course you were justified in these feelings. You were always justified, weren't you? "My boss is just a horrible person"; "He just doesn't understand my needs"; or "He won't let me talk about Jesus on the job". It always amazes me when people say, "I need to go to work for a Christian company. I just can't stand it in this godless environment anymore."

Well I guess God will have to find someone else to get those heathens saved, since you don't want to be bothered or put out by their lack of moral fiber. Are you kidding me?

What do you expect? They're sinners, just like you were before you received Christ's sacrifice for the forgiveness of your sin.

Too many times we bail, just before the blessing. We go A.W.O.L. (Absent With Out Leave) and completely miss out on the blessing God had planned and finally understanding the reason God placed you where He did. Think about it. What an honor, He trusts you! God chose you to bring the Gospel message to people that need Jesus! Stop trying to constantly change your circumstances and start following the Holy Spirit that He might use you to change your world.

We feed these cycles of discontentment and then wonder why our kids are the way they are. We've set them up for failure and it's time to stop.

"It's about the passion to be a follower…"

We need to get to the place that we would rather starve to death in the center of God's will, than to be out of His will feasting on the sins of pleasantness for a season. Naomi had heard that God had visited His people and provided bread for them, so she made a commitment to return to the Land of God's Provision.

Upon seeing the resolve of her mother inlaw, Ruth also made a commitment, to forsake all and follow her.

Over the course of history we see a push to strive for the role of leader. We are made to feel that any position less than that of a leader makes us substandard. In reality it's all about being one who follows well. As Christians it's about the passion to be a follower, a follower of Christ, and a follower of those who walk in His ways!

When Ruth saw her mother-in-law, she saw the anguish and the pain she was going through, but she also saw a woman who was determined to return to her home in Judah. Namoi had nothing there and no one waiting for her, but nevertheless she was returning to the place of God's Provision. Ruth had no idea that God was preparing to use her in such a wonderful way.

As Naomi shared her intentions with them Ruth clung to her and said, "I will follow!" "I will go wherever you go; I will live wherever you live; I will adopt your people, and your traditions. Your God will now be my God; wherever you die, there will I die and there is where I will also be buried." God sees and honors Ruth's commitment and immediately begins a redemptive work that will end up including her in the bloodline of King David and inevitably in the lineage that will bring forth God's only begotten Son, Jesus Christ, the Messiah.

Ruth 1:6-7

Then she arose with her daughters in law, that she might return from the country of Moab: for she had heard in the country of Moab how that the Lord had visited his people in giving them bread. Wherefore she went forth out of the place where she was, and her two daughters in law with her; and they went on the way to return unto the land of Judah.

There is a key to redemption tucked away in these verses that we may miss if we read it too quickly. Although Ruth made the decision to follow Naomi, Naomi first had to make the decision to follow God. Naomi was the initiator, she was intentional in her actions. Verse six says that she arose to return to Judah, and then in verse seven it continues to tell us that she put feet to her faith.

God used the bleakness of her current situation to prepare her to embark on her redemptive journey. This was not a move motivated by circumstance, but rather driven by necessity. The necessity to once again be in the center of God's will. Naomi chose to look to God for the fulfillment of His promised provision, rather than remain in the substandard place of human solution. With this decision came an immediate reward, a daughter who would become God's instrument to redeem Elimelech's family back into the heirship of Israel.

The effects of poor decisions still haunt you today. Feelings of guilt overwhelm you as you look at the lives of those who are broken and seemingly unfixable because of your decisions. But thankfully God's grace is revealed again in the words of Jesus when He said in Luke 18:27,

"The things that are impossible with men are possible with God."

Don't be an Elimelech. Don't be moved by circumstances. Don't leave a legacy of regret and bondage to fear. The decisions you make today will impact the future in ways you can't begin to imagine. Call upon the Holy Spirit to guide you into making right choices, reversing generational curses and changing the future of your family. In spite of your past, it's time for a change! It's time to positively impact eternity.

"The decisions you make today will impact the future in ways you can't begin to imagine."

I am living proof that God is able to reverse the curse of sin. I was eternally Hell bound. Eternally! Nothing could stop me from reaching my eternal destination. I was going to Hell like a locomotive, fast and furious! Every one of us on this planet is in the same situation. Our souls are destined to eternal damnation.

It's like a gravitational force that attracts the fallen soul of mankind and pulls it into its clutches like iron is drawn to a magnet. But in the midst of that stream, God chose to place the body of His son Jesus Christ as a net to catch all those who will trust in Him. If God can do that, there is nothing impossible or irreversible for Him. How bleak is the picture you've painted of your life with the brush strokes of thoughtless actions birthed out of your poor decisions?

"There's still hope!"

Own your responsibility, repent of the things you are guilty of, confess them to God and accept His forgiveness through Jesus Christ. Salvation is not based on your works, but upon the completed works of Christ. The only requirement after you're saved is submission to Christ!

Abandon your own personal agenda, and live solely for Him. Yield to His Word, be led by His Spirit and walk in His ways! Fully submitted from your waking up in the morning, to your going to bed at night. From our checking in at the job, to your coming home to your family. From the way you treat your spouse, to the way you influence your children. In everything, fully submitted!

There is still hope! Still hope for those who have been hurt by poor examples, for those who have been affected by poor decisions. There's still hope because we serve a God of reconciliation, a God of restoration, a God of redemption. He has chosen to provide forgiveness and healing for you and for all who have been left in your wake of destructive behaviors. He paid the ultimate price for you by offering His sinless Son, Jesus Christ, to cover your sinfulness.Until the final day when you breathe your last breath, there is still hope if you repent of your sins and place your trust in Christ.

I wish we could understand that submission is easier than we think it is. If I go to shake someone's hand and he pulls back from me I wonder to myself, "Why is he resisting me? All I am trying to do is extend a mutual act of friendship. No requirements attached, just an extension of my love toward him." But once he learns to trust me, then he yields to my hand and submits to my gesture. He actually anticipates and reaches out to welcome it. It then becomes a mutually beneficial connection.

That is all God wants you to do, just submit to His gesture of love. Jesus Christ is declaring this Word to you today:

Matthew 11:28

"Come to me, all of you who are tired and over-burdened and I will give you rest."

He's inviting you to come into His presence, to relax, and learn to submit to His love for you. Stop making decisions that are having negative generational impacts on you and your family for years to come; decisions that are taking you out of His will and robbing you of His promises all because you are not patient enough or trusting enough for Him to complete His work. Today, decide to follow Christ!

"Stop making decisions that…are taking you out of His will and robbing you of His promises…"

The Father is crying out to us through His Word and by His Holy Spirit! The end of the world is coming! The Son of God's return is drawing closer than we realize. Look around you, the decadence of evil is rising and God's name is being blasphemed by those who once held it dear.

There is no more time to waste trying to do things on our own, turn to Christ, turn to Christ! Follow the lead of the Moabitess servant Ruth, leave your past behind, your false gods, your earthly treasures, your inappropriate relationships.

Cling to Jesus, and watch God create for you and the generations to come, a bright hope and a promising future! He will use you to fulfill His purposes to bring this message of Salvation to all the world. All of this because He is the God of Redemption, and He will redeem those who pursue after Him!

Psalm 24:1-10

"The earth is the Lord's, and the fulness thereof; the world, and they that dwell therein. For he hath founded it upon the seas, and established it upon the floods. Who shall

ascend into the hill of the Lord? or who shall stand in his holy place? He that hath clean hands, and a pure heart; who hath not lifted up his soul unto vanity, nor sworn deceitfully. He shall receive the blessing from the Lord, and righteousness from the God of his salvation. This is the generation of them that seek him, that seek thy face, O Jacob. Selah. Lift up your heads, O ye gates; and be ye lift up, ye everlasting doors; and the King of glory shall come in. Who is this King of glory? The Lord strong and mighty, the Lord mighty in battle. Lift up your heads, O ye gates; even lift them up, ye everlasting doors; and the King of glory shall come in. Who is this King of glory? The Lord of hosts, he is the King of glory. Selah."

I have no intention of wasting my time building another generation of positive thinkers or prosperity seekers. I cry out for God to use me to raise up Christ-followers of all generations.

Today, may we be the generations united by the power of the cross, redeemed by His resurrection, and empowered by the baptism of the Holy Spirit. May we set our hearts to seek God, to know Him and to submit to His voice, intently listening and intentionally following, as He leads us on our redemptive journey to live as Christ lived and save as Christ saved.

CHAPTER 4

MAN'S SOLUTION VS GOD'S PROVISION

Names say a lot, not only about the person, but also about the individual who named the person. It can reveal what they might have been going through in their life at the time of the child's birth.

Let's start with Elimelech. Elimelech means 'God of the king'. What a name! Can you imagine that? Every time someone calls your name you're reminded that your God is the ultimate in power and that He is above all authority, even over that of the king! No matter what you are going through, somebody calls your name and it's a constant reminder, 'God is the Supreme Ruler!'.

Every time you sign your name on a check, 'God is over all authority!'. Every time the utility bill arrives in the mailbox the name on the front reminds you that, 'God is in charge!'. What a great reminder, that God is in control.

Naomi's name means 'Pleasant and Beautiful'. When someone calls out to you they are saying, "Hey, 'Pleasant and Beautiful'. Wow, I think a person could get used to that!

Elimelech and Naomi had two sons. One was named Mahlon, and the other Chilion. Mahlon means 'diseased and afflicted'. Chilion means 'destructive failure'. Wow, Dad, Mom! What were you thinking?! Why would they choose such defeated names for their sons? Then it dawned on me, in their day, the father usually assigned the names of the children. Although the mother may have had input, the father was the main influence.

It is my personal belief that the names chosen for their two sons were a direct reflection of the spiritual duress of Elimelech's heart. The names he chose for his sons reveal that the Fear of the Lord had left Elimelech long before he ever left his homeland. He had lost hope, vision and no longer believed the promises of God. The sin of doubt and disbelief don't just occur, but rather they slowly and methodically dig their claws into their victims over a process of time.

Once in Moab their two sons then married Moabite women. One was named Orpah, meaning 'Stiff-necked'. Wow, talk about flattering! Maybe her parents had an argument the day she was born. The other, Ruth, whose name means 'Companion and Friend'. Wow, what a wonderful identity to place on your child, one that would actually come to pass.

In chapter 1, verse 6, after the death of Naomi's husband and two sons we come to the part of the story where she decides to return home to Bethlehem-Judah. Her daughters-in-law try to follow her yet she refuses to allow them.

Orpah heeds Naomi's words when she tells her to return to her mother's home, but Ruth does not. We learn in verse 14 that Ruth clave to Naomi, she joined herself to her mother-in-law, then proceeded to beg her not to send her away and make her go home. Naomi finally agrees for Ruth to accompany her, but can offer no promise of a better life.

Ruth 1:19-22

So they two went until they came to Beth–lehem. And it came to pass, when they were come to Beth–lehem, that all the city was moved about them, and they said, Is this Naomi? And she said unto them, Call me not Naomi, call me Mara: for the Almighty hath dealt very bitterly with me. I went out full, and the Lord hath brought me home again empty: why then call ye me Naomi, seeing the Lord hath testified against me, and the Almighty hath afflicted me? So Naomi returned, and Ruth the Moabitess, her daughter in law, with her, which returned out of the country of Moab: and they came to Beth–lehem in the beginning of barley harvest.

The entire city was amazed when the saw Naomi as she and Ruth arrived in Bethlehem. It had been years since her family's exodus and they wanted to see how she was doing.

As they began to call her by name, she quickly rebukes them and declares that she has renamed herself 'Mara', which means 'bitter and worn', an external expression of her internal condition. She then blames the Lord for her state of existence and says, "I left Bethlehem wealthy, yet I am returning destitute. Obviously the Lord has afflicted me."

Wait a minute! Who afflicted who? I understand you're upset with your unfortunate circumstances, but why are you blaming God for your 'self-affliction'?

"...why are you blaming God for your 'self-affliction'?

One thing we need to clarify at this point in our story is that there is a difference between a 'true statement' and a 'statement of truth'. A true statement just acknowledges the fact that someone made a specific statement, but it doesn't mean that the content or context of what they said was a statement of truth. I can say that I have blonde hair and blue eyes. Yes, it is true that I made this statement, but it is not a statement of truth. But if I said, "I have dark brown hair with lots of gray highlights and dark brown eyes." this is not only a true statement, but it is also a statement of truth.

We need to be more careful with our words. I'm sure we have all blamed God for something that had nothing to do with Him, but rather had everything to do with our personal decisions.

It is a true statement that Naomi said that the Lord has afflicted her, but I personally do not believe it is a statement of truth. As we have discovered, the reason she was not in the realm of blessing any more, had nothing to do with God, and everything to do with her late husband. Elimelech had made some very poor decisions for his family and they suffered the consequences. These types of heart issues begin to form our identity.

Remember that Elimelech's name means 'God of the King'. This should have served as a constant reminder to

Elimelech that God is in control; He is God over my circumstances, regardless of what I am seeing or what I am going through. It was a form of identity that his father had given him to remember to whom He belonged.

If you have accepted God's gift of salvation through Jesus Christ, then you are a child of God. He has given you an identity that is now officially in Jesus Christ! Your Heavenly Father has everything under His control. All that is required of us is to stay focused on Him and surrender to His will.

But how many times have you lost focus? How many times have you looked at the famine in the land, and quickly forgotten God's promises? How many times have you allowed your circumstances to dictate your decisions? I can answer that for myself, "Too many times!"

During this time in history, the age of the Judges was coming to an end. The slogan was, "Do what is right in your own sight." A decadence of moral failure was sweeping throughout the nation of Israel. It was time for God's people to repent and cry out to Him for forgiveness, but instead they turned to their own solutions.

Elimelech started out in the Land of Promise, but he lost focus. His own name resounded, "God is over all authority; He is over all circumstance; His power is over all!" But Elimelech had grown numb to the proclamation of this statement of truth and allowed his heart to grow callous toward God and His ability to deliver what He had promised.

Elimelech had become a product of the hopelessness of his environment and must have felt pressured by the situation. He chose to leave the land of Promise and walk out of God's blessing, walking out of God's will for his life. Why?

Because the circumstances surrounding him became more real to him than the 'God of the king'. He lost sight of his identity. When you allow hopelessness to take over, you assume the identity of your environment.

"When you allow hopelessness to take over, you assume the identity of your environment."

Sometimes God uses circumstances to prompt us to move in a certain direction because we either aren't hearing Him or we have grown too comfortable. When it's God's prompting, there will be peace and He will be glorified. But when we do the prompting, chaos enters the scene and destruction is soon to follow. When we think God hasn't solved our problem, we assume that He must be waiting for us to fix it.

Elimelech must have assumed that he needed to step in since He didn't see God's hand in his situation. So being moved by circumstance, he makes the decision to leave the land of Promise, the land of 'God's Provision' and seek out 'Man's Solution'.

When you are in God's will, He will take care of you. This doesn't mean that everything is going to go perfectly, or even the way you think it should. This is not a get rich quick scheme; this is not a modern day prosperity message that sells the buyer a self-centered product and promises you can have whatever you want whenever you want it; this isn't about thinking enough positive thoughts to remove all doubt then pulling the big handle in the sky and hitting the jackpot. Woohoo! All of your dreams come true, all you've ever wanted, with no pain, no suffering and nothing required of you! No, this is about the Provision of God.

Meeting life's needs and essentials so you can be prepared and fully equipped to step into the supernatural, and go preach the gospel; to reach out to the people who are lost in your family, in your city, in your nation, and in your world, and see them saved by the redemptive work of Jesus Christ. Within God's will, is His provision to equip us to complete the task at hand. But outside of His will, in the midst of our solution, all we will find is disappointment, destruction and eventually death.

When Elimelech decided to take his family to the land of Moab, he removed them from the land of 'God's Provision' and placed them into the land of 'Man's Solution'. Our decisions always involve someone else. Who followed Elimelech? His wife and his two sons. Your decisions create an eternal impact, not only on your life, but on the lives of those around you.

"Your decisions create an eternal impact, not only on your life, but on the lives of those around you."

With that in mind, we turn our attention back to Naomi. Elimelech makes the decision to move to Moab and she follows with her two sons tagging along behind. Upon arrival in Moab, Elimelech must have thought to himself, "Now we will be taken care of. I've fixed it; I've taken care of everything! My family will be fine." He must have been so proud of himself. I mean think about it, he fixed what God obviously couldn't. Oh yeah, he did it all right! He did it all by himself, without any help from God. What a valiant decision he made to walk out of God's Provision and into Man's Solution. I'm sure everything will be just fine now... Elimelech dies. Oops, didn't see that one comin'!

What? He does what? He dies?! Okay, that was definitely not in the plan! You know Lord, 'my plan', the one that fixed what Your plan couldn't!

So where does this leave Naomi? Widowed in a foreign land, a single mother with two sons. Her sons meet and marry Moabite women. Naomi must have thought, "Well, now that my sons are married, I can live with my sons and help when they start having my grandkids."

It's obvious that Elimelech not only made a very bad decision moving his family to Moab, but made an equally bad decision not teaching his sons about their heritage, the Law of God, and the religious traditions of his people. His lack of instruction is revealed in their choice to marry Moabite women instead of women from Israel. This was unacceptable. God gave a direct commandment to Israel not to take wives of the foreign nations due to the fact that these women would lead their husbands into idolatry and away from God (Exodus 39:16).

Elimelech seemed to impart no Fear of the Lord, and instill no desire in his sons to return to their homeland of Bethlehem-Judah and re-secure their inheritance after their father's death. When you're out of God's will, He is usually not the favored topic of choice. After you decide to walk out of God's provision, you really don't want to talk about Him. You know in your heart you've sinned, so just the mention of God's name brings feelings of guilt so to protect your pride you begin the slippery slope of justification.

In spite of its bad reputation, guilt is actually a wonderful thing, it takes you to a crossroad. When you're confronted with guilt, you can do one of two things. You can either yield to the convicting power of the Holy Spirit, humble yourself, admit your failure, be forgiven and follow Christ; or you can harden your heart, justify your actions and be dragged down a road of condemnation. Either way it brings you face to face with a choice, which demands a decision. Just one decision that will chart the course of your destiny for years to come.

The two boys, now men, marry two Moabite women and now everything is going to be all right. Mahlon and Chilion die. Wow! A triple whammy! What was that all about? I'm no rocket scientist, but something just doesn't feel right.

To summarize for those who are taking notes, it is never a good idea to walk out of 'God's Provision' into 'Man's Solution'! Elimelech was dead and soon after his two sons died also. All total they leave three widows with no children. Ouch!

"It is never a good idea to walk out of 'God's Provision' into 'Man's Solution'!"

Think about this, there are no government-subsidized programs. Naomi is a widow in a male driven culture. She is stuck in a foreign land, she is destitute, she has no husband, no sons, no income, no provision, no family, no friends, no hope, and not even a promise to be redeemed to her former position in her homeland.

You want to talk about a dark situation?! There was nothing but a big black hole right in front of her and no way of getting around it. This is exactly where Naomi found herself, and to top it off she's left with two widowed daughters-in-laws who aren't quite sure what to do now and are looking to Naomi for direction. Elimelech's decision created a domino effect and it looked like the last domino was about to fall, affecting everyone he had once loved.

I stand in awe when someone, in their infinite wisdom, blurts out, "It's my decision! It only affects me. It's no one else's business!" This reasoning equates to the epitome of a mid 16th century Latin word, stupidus, also known in English as 'stupid'! This expression has been swallowed hook line and sinker by Christians who have allowed themselves to be 'affected' by society rather than being the 'effector' on society.

It reminds me of the smoker who says, "It's my Decision. It only affects me!" As they blow the smoky residue of their decision into the communal air. Or the person who can't take the brief minute necessary to toss their empty water bottle into a recycling bin and then blames everyone else for the environmental issues the earth is facing. Or how about the lie we've been fed by a society that robs babies the right to live when they ignorantly chant, "My body, my choice!". What about the body of the little person inside who was conceived by no choice of its own.

Your decisions do impact other people, ALWAYS! Thank God for His unfailing mercy and grace that forgives us of our past sins and failures, and restores us back to a right-standing with Him. Let us return to Him with a repentant heart and call upon Christ for forgiveness.

As well as the losses already mentioned, Elimelech's decision threatened to remove his family's name from the heirship of Israel, forever. There were no more sons to carry on the family name. Elimelech's lineage had come to an abrupt halt. All of this because of one decision, just one!

"Only in the land of God's Provision will you ever enter into the Land of Promise."

As Naomi sits in the depths of her despair, she begins to think of her homeland. "What if?" She must have been saying to herself, "What if we had stayed in the land of Promise? What if we would have waited on God for His Provision? What if we would have raised our sons in the instruction of our God, according to His statutes? What if they would have married women of Israel?" "What if?" "What if?" The questions were unanswerable, haunting her mind every minute of the day as she sat in the thick darkness of hopelessness longing to see even a flicker of hope, but there was none.

Elimelech was moved by circumstance. In contrast we see Naomi being moved by necessity. Not a necessity to find another 'solution', but to return to God's 'provision'. It's hard to wait on answers, but many times God's answer is, "Wait and watch! Wait upon Me and you will behold My glory. Stand in awe of My presence and I will take you where I want you to go."

Naomi comes to a point when she realizes that there is nothing for her in Moab; there is nothing for her outside of God's will. The God of Provision is in the Land of Promise. She had been living in a land with no promise, only death and destruction, and she was done. At that moment she made an intentional decision to leave the land of 'Man's Solution' and return to the land of 'God's Provision'. Only in the land of God's Provision will you ever enter into the Land of Promise.

We rarely calculate the impact of our decisions. When you make decisions people will follow. What happened when Naomi made a decision? Other people followed. If you make right decisions, God will place those in your life that will help you on your journey. They will help pray for you and support you.

I am not talking necessarily about financially and physically, those things come as you continue to follow God's direction and the needs arise, I am more so talking about spiritually. The inner support provided by the Holy Spirit through others to lift you up and encourage you. This is where Ruth comes into play.

"…if you make the right decisions, God will place those in your life that will help you on your journey."

Ruth had nothing to offer her mother-in-law. No money, no home, and no guarantee of gainful employment. But she gave Naomi all she had to give, a spirit of encouragement and support. She boldly stepped out in faith and made a commitment to Naomi, "I am with you where you go. I do not fully understand what you are talking about, or where you're going, but I will be here beside you. I will serve your God. Your God will be my God. Where you die I will die. I want your people to be my people. I am here to support you and lift you up. I am here to be with you." God provided this type of support for Naomi because she made a 'God decision'.

Beginning her journey home and still unsure of her standing with God, Naomi is convinced that He has dealt treacherously with her and adopts a new name, Mara, which means bitterness. A true reflection of the hopelessness of her condition, yet even still she finds herself driven to return to her homeland; a return that provides no promise of anything but ridicule by those who watched her family walk out of Judah and into Moab so many years before.

Elimelech died after his decision, leaving his wife a widow and eventually childless having to bury her two sons. She was homeless and hopeless. But Naomi's decision restored life, hope and redemption. Little did she know that her young Moabite daughter-in-law would be the vessel used by God to redeem her family's inheritance and secure their place in the lineage of the Messiah. Ruth supported Naomi in what is the darkest time in her life; she stood by her side as an encourager and God rewarded her for it.

Have you ever had someone stand with you in those times? If so, why don't you put the book down for a minute, send them a text, a quick email or even a brief phone call. Tell them you appreciate the fact that they stood with you during that dark time in your life when you needed extra support, and a special friend.

Naomi must have begun to teach Ruth the ways of God, pouring into her the teachings of her heritage. Ruth listens intently accepting all that her mother-in-law instructs her to do. In the same way, if we would stop continually criticizing those who are our authorities in Christ and instead commit ourselves to them; to encourage them and support them, those pastors and leaders would begin to pour themselves into us and impart to us what God has entrusted to them.

Through this faithfulness, you and I will enter into our own personal revelation of God and embrace Him as Holy and Righteous, full of Mercy and Grace. At that time it will no longer be about what He can do for us, but it will be all about how we can honor Him through our radical commitment and sold out service.

As their journey progressed, you can see how Naomi had obviously shared with Ruth about the importance of preserving the family genealogy; about how the promises of God came to God's people. She eventually explained to Ruth the obligations of the law regarding the care of relatives. She was teaching Ruth God's ways, and Ruth was learning. Although she was a Moabite, her heart was for God and honoring His ways.

CHAPTER 5

POSITIONED FOR PROVIDENCE

Ruth 2:1

And Naomi had a kinsman of her husband's, a mighty man (warrior, chief, valiant, brave, strong, giant-great man) of wealth (efficient, valor, powerful in possessions, as well as in military might), of the family of Elimelech; and his name was Boaz. And Ruth the Moabitess said unto Naomi, Let me now go to the field, and glean ears of corn after him in whose sight I shall find grace. And she said unto her, Go, my daughter. And she went, and came, and gleaned in the field after the reapers: and her hap was to light on the part of the field belonging unto Boaz, who was of the kindred of Elimelech.

Elimelech is an example of what happens when someone interferes with God. He was motivated by circumstance and left the land of God's provision to go to the land of man's solution. Others followed his lead. He dies. His sons, seemingly untrained in the ways of God, marry outside the children of Israel and then die themselves leaving two widows, childless.

His wife is left destitute, bitter, discontent, with no income, no hope, no provision, no government-subsidized programs, and no promise of redemption to her former state of prominence in her homeland. It was a domino effect. The decision that Elimelech made affected everyone around him and almost completely removed his family tree from the inheritance of God's people.

"But God!"

But God intervenes! Naomi was motivated by necessity. She was in a land without promise. Her family had died. Moab, the land of Man's Solution, had taken everything and left her with nothing. She made the decision to leave the land of man's solution and headed back to God's Provision and someone followed her lead.

In her decision to return, she is rewarded with life and hope through the accompaniment of her son's widow, Ruth. Naomi's decision affected everyone in her generation and in the generations to come. One decision took them completely 'out' of the blessing. Yet one decision could reclaimed their inheritance and secure their position 'in' the blessing.

Naomi made the decision to return to God's provision, but Naomi was not the only one involved in this process. Even though she was the original one who made the initial decision that would begin the redemptive effect, others had to follow that same trend of right decisions in order to ensure its fulfillment.

There are always others involved? Your father may have made the decision to accept Jesus Christ as his savior, break generational curses and devote his life to serving God. This is only the first phase of a multilevel decision. Now you come along. Your daddy made a good decision, but now it is your turn. You can't go to heaven on his coattail. Will you make the right decision to give your life to Jesus Christ?

As good as it is that you make your decision to follow Christ and as wonderfully as God may use you throughout you life, your child must be faced with the same decision for themselves as well. The more generations that make the right decision, the stronger that decision gets and the greater the effect is on the generations to come. Each generation having a more firm foundation from which to build because of the decisions made by those who have went on before.

You see, it is one thing to make a decision, and it is another thing to back it up and perform it. You know what I am talking about. Every January 1st, people begin the cycle of New Year's resolutions. Call it whatever you want to, but regardless what you call it, you are making promises to yourself. It is one thing to make those promises, and another thing all together to perform them.

It can be the difference between living in the land of God's provision or continuing to wander aimlessly somewhere outside the boarders of the city wallowing in man's solution. We can decide to leave the land of man's solution, but that doesn't mean we will automatically enter into the land of God's provision. Ruth 1:22, says,

> *"So Naomi returned, and Ruth the Moabitess, her daughter-in-law, with her, which returned out of the country of Moab: and they came to Bethlehem in the beginning of barley harvest."*

It was Naomi's decision to leave man's solution and by doing this, she positioned herself for God's Providence, a place where we meet God's divine intervention. Naomi and Ruth were on the road home, but there was still no redemption, there was still no provision, there was still no evidence of a promise that would be fulfilled. What now? What were they supposed to do?

It was that time again. Yes, it was time for another decision. Another decision had to be made in order to continue the flow of this redemptive process. The ball had been set into motion, but someone had to keep it going. It was now Ruth's turn to make a decision. Every time you make a decision, you solidify the next generation's opportunity to follow your example in making that same decision in the same way you did, whether for good or for bad.

"Every time you make a decision, you solidify the next generation's opportunity to follow your example in making that same decision in the same way you did..."

There are generations of people that wonder why they keep making the same bad decisions? It's because their father made the same decision, their father's father made the same, their father's father's father started it and nobody turned to God for the strength to break it. They either don't realize they can cry out to God to break it, or they have decided that it's easer just to settle for status quo. News flash - "God does not live in status quo."

So now it was Ruth's turn to step out.

Ruth 2:2

And Ruth the Moabitess said unto Naomi, Let me now go to the field, and glean ears of corn after him in whose sight I shall find grace. And she said unto her, Go my daughter.

Ruth took a bold step of faith towards a God that she did not know personally, except through the eyes and life of Naomi. Will this God truly provide for her and for her mother-in-law? The instantaneous result of that decision is in the continuance of the redemption process.

We see the immediate effect in Ruth 2:3

And she went, and came, and gleaned in the field after the reapers: and her hap was to light on a part of the field belonging unto Boaz, who was of the kindred of Elimelech.

Boaz gave direct orders to his servants regarding the provision afforded to Ruth. They were to let her gather from the good that was left, drink from their water, eat their food, and stay close to his handmaidens for protection. This is a miracle!

You see, we are from America where our country's theme has been not only to receive the foreigner, but to care for them. So we have a hard time understanding a culture that would not do that. Because of Ruth's decision to trust the God of Israel, she was able to leave Boaz' field that day praising Him for His Provision and thanking Him for a very personal experience with Naomi's God.

By chance she came to Boaz's field? Go figure! How in the world did that happen? I mean, of all the fields that she could have went to in that land. Of all the people she could have gleaned after, in a time of harvest when everyone is working. But by 'chance', she just happened to stumble upon Boaz' property? Really, by chance?

Some might consider this coincidence or happenstance. But in actuality, this was only the beginning of God's providence. This was the divine intervention of God to honor Ruth's step of faith, to save his people, and to redeem the bloodline of Elimelech, the same man who lost sight of God's provision.

Ruth no longer had to rely on an experience rehearsed from someone else. She had been hearing experiences from Naomi for quite awhile. It's one thing to hear someone else's testimony secondhand, and a completely different thing to hear it from the person that was actually there. To have them share their own personal experience creates a passion and a drive that goes beyond anything that you could ever relay. This is why the Holy Spirit has to live inside the believer.

If I try to testify of God's Word in my own strength, it would be a dead letter. I have to have the Witness in me, the Holy Spirit, and He will speak for Himself. He speaks with passion and with power about the mercy of a loving God. Ruth was now able to say for herself, "I have now seen God work first hand on my behalf."

She returned to her mother-in-law with a zeal that she had never experienced before. Naomi's decision had positioned them for providence, but Ruth's decision took them into the heart of God's provision.

"Naomi's decision had positioned them for providence, but Ruth's decision took them into the heart of God's provision."

Think about it. In one day, God had begun to restore what the past decade had wiped out. But God! But God provided Boaz! You may wonder why Naomi was so excited. Ruth walks in after a long day in the fields and Naomi asks, "Where did you get this food Ruth? Where have you been gleaning? Where have you been working?"

The gleaners were used to picking up the leftovers. But if you remember, Boaz said, leave some of the "good stuff" and do not rebuke her for taking it. By the time she got through pounding out what she had gleaned, she had brought home enough grain to feed two people for ten days. Gleaners are used to living one day at a time.

Did you see what God did? Just arriving into town and He already provided food and income. Boaz told Ruth that she was to glean with his laborers through the entire harvest. In one day, Ruth gleaned ten days worth of grain.

God provided not only enough to eat, but extra to trade for clothing, shelter, and other necessities. God provided provision and protection to a foreigner in a foreign land. He restored hope to Naomi by providing Ruth with favor in the eyes of Boaz, a man of influence and wealth.

"Ruth made a decision to do something where she was."

Ruth made a decision to do something where she was. How many times in your life have you been positioned for providence? Prepped and ready for God's divine intervention to begin to work mightily in your life. A place where God can fulfill His desires and accomplish His purposes through you, but you never take the step. It's like going in for pre-op, getting ready for surgery. All of the tests have been done. Everything is prepared. You are ready to go. You have been positioned for a successful surgery, all you have to do is walk into the operating room, yet you choose to miss the appointment.

How many times have people in your life made decisions and personal sacrifices that positioned you for providence? How about the mothers that pray earnestly for their children? By their personal sacrifice, they place their children in a position for providence. My mother and my father positioned me for providence by their prayers and provision, and for that I will be forever grateful.

I remember when I would ride the kindergarten school bus. As we pulled away, I would look out the window at our little apartment building wondering what mom does when I leave? One morning I said, "Mom, what do you do when I go to school?" I mean, what do moms do when we aren't there to give them a reason to live, right? My mom looked at me and said, "Son, as soon as you get on the bus, I start to pray for you. When I walk in the door I go straight to the couch in the living room and kneel before God to pray for you."

From that day on, every time I would pull away in the big yellow school bus, I would look at the apartment building and imagine my mother kneeling in our living room praying for me. My mother made a decision to position me for God's providence and it impacted my life for eternity.

"My mother made a decision to position me for God's providence and it impacted my life for eternity."

Both my parents made many personal sacrifices to help position me for providence. But there came a time when I had to make a personal decision in order to continue the redemptive flow they had begun. Many times people have supported you, whether physically or prayerfully. They made a decision to set you up for the providence of God, yet you may have failed to take the step.

Life gets out of hand, we get busy, we lose track of time. We find ourselves saying things like, "I'm going to give my heart to Jesus as soon as I get my life straightened out.", "I'm going to start taking my family to church as soon as we get things under control.", "I will go to a marriage counselor once I convince my spouse that they need help.", or "I'll start a budget as soon as I have enough money." If that's your thought pattern then your most likely headed for divorce court, bankruptcy and will be spiritually dead before you know what hit you.

Many times we fail to make the one decision to take that one step to follow God's direction. Then years later you wonder why nothing ever seemed to work out, and why your life never impacted eternity. All because you chose to wander outside the walls of God's providence.

CHAPTER 6
ABANDONING
SELF-SUFFICIENCY

You may have made the decision to leave the land of "man's solution", also known as the land of self-sufficiency, but you never quite took the step to position yourself for providence. To go there would have required something of you, something that you weren't ready to give. Heaven forbid you may have to suffer, feel pain, or experience personal loss. So your failure to step into a position of providence was actually a decision to wander in limbo outside of God's provision.

You find yourself in a place where nothing seems real. Nothing is definite and definitely nothing is clear. In order to fully enter into the land of his provision, you must position yourself by leaving everything self-sufficient outside the gates.

"...to fully enter into the land of his provision, you must position yourself by leaving everything self-sufficient outside the gates."

I need to make sure you are really hearing what I just said. I don't know who raised you, where you came from or even your background. I do know that from where I came from self-sufficiency used to be considered a good thing and in theory it is in regards to supporting yourself and your family. That is until we get prideful and begin to think that self-sufficiency means we can do it alone.

It was common for men not to give God all the credit for their success, because after all, "God may have given me the job, but I actually did do the work myself." Right? A prideful self-sufficiency will hinder us from ever walking into the provision of God's fullness.

We can honestly say that Ruth was self-sufficient. She took the initiative, she made the decision to follow Naomi, to leave her family, and even to work in the fields. But in all of this Ruth never once touted a prideful self-sufficiency. She unwittingly allowed a God that she did not know to chart her steps and in the end gave the praise to the only One who deserves the credit.

In reality Ruth was not self-sufficient at all! She was stepping out in faith. Knowing that she had nothing to offer. She had no protection, no reputation, no status, no inheritance, no home, and no rights. Just talk to the women in the middle east if you're serious about understanding what Ruth was dealing with at the time. She was a foreigner in a foreign land. There was no self-sufficiency in her. If she would have fallen into the wrong hands, she could have been killed, sold into slavery, or simply banished from the city and left destitute.

Ruth was anything but self-sufficient. She willfully chose to place her trust in the sufficiency of a God who loved His people and would take care of them at any cost rather than trust in the familiar. Now that is true sufficiency!

Personal sovereignty is not welcomed and cannot exist within the boundless mercies of God's eternal grace, power and provision. God will not help you in a world where you are in control. You must release your world and come into His, because in your world, YOU are still king. In your world, YOU still call the shots. In your world, YOU are still seeking man's solution through your self-sufficiency. Let it go, it is dragging you down. Your self-sufficiency is keeping you from entering into God's provision.

"God will not help you in a world where you are in control."

Through the completed work of his son Jesus Christ, and the love that He has shown you, God has placed you, right now, in a position for providence. Because of God's mercy and the prayers, support, and love of those He has placed in your life, you have been positioned for providence. God gave His only begotten Son to die for you on a cross and to rise from the grave so that your sins would be forgiven; that you would be reinstated as a child of God. By trusting in Christ you have been placed in a position for providence.

Will you take the next step? Will you abandon your self-sufficiency? Your belief that God helps those who help themselves? Your pride, your arrogance, your habits, your vices, your religious notions based on the traditions of man? Your possessions, your relationships? Your good works and your securities? The reality is this – God helps those who humble themselves. Humble yourselves in the sight of the Lord and he shall lift you up (1 Peter 5:6). Repent of your sin of self-sufficiency, humble yourself before the Almighty King, trust in Christ as your Savior and step into providence!

Interestingly enough, the provision that God brought to Ruth, all began to come into reality when she entered into the what? That's right, when she entered into the "harvest" field. (Ruth 2:2)

God released to Ruth the provision that He had reserved for her 'after' she entered into the harvest field. You see, when she had humbled herself to perform the menial task of gleaning the fields, taking the left overs, that which nobody else wanted and doing the clean up, she found herself right smack in the middle of God's provision. This was not a coincidence. What happens during harvest? It's a four-letter word that starts with a "W". Yep, W-O-R-K! Work is what's happening during harvest. From the moment harvest begins there is no down time. Only a small window of opportunity is available to gather the crop before it begins to over-ripen, spoil and lose its value.

When Jesus was discussing the harvest of souls with His disciples He never said that the harvest is over. I can't find once in scripture where He said we are to stop praying for the harvest, or that we are to stop being laborers in His harvest field. Yet so many times we are tempted to sit idly by and not enter into His work with Him.

We need to clearly understand that God's provision lives right smack in the middle of His work. God blesses those who are consumed with His business, completely reliant on His sufficiency instead of your own. His work should be a natural product of your life. His work begins when you pour God's love out onto your family, and on those

He as entrusted to you. His work continues when you walk through the grocery store and the clerk actually looks forward to you coming through their line, because they feel God's presence, even if they can't explain it. They know that you are always willing to pray for them. His work is when you wake up to the reality that your life is to be lived for Him, you are no longer your own. So you offer yourself to Him as a living, breathing sacrificial witness of His love and forgiveness.

"…God's provision lives right smack in the middle of His work."

When we join God in His work, our primary business and responsibility is to our family. I heard it said by an individual on the radio one day while driving through our town, "Marriage must be the permanent priority relationship in family". Wow, that resonated in my spirit the entire day! I still use this principle today as key in helping me strive for a successful marriage and family life.

Husbands and wives are responsible to care for, love, nurture and build each other up in Christ. There should be no sweeter earthly place for solace than in the presence of a Christ-focused marriage (Eph 5). I would not be the man that I am today if God had not given me the wife He did. In addition to everything else I owe Him, I am forever thankful for the woman of God He blessed me with to insure I would continue on the path to becoming all He has called me to be.

As parents, our responsibility is to train up our children in the way that they should go so they will not turn away from it (Eph 6). Establishing their faith in Christ at a young age so when they go into the school system, which denies God and fosters rebellion, witchcraft, and the perversions of the world, they will be equipped by you, their parents, to stand for Christ in this ever present darkness. We are to protect and equip our children and teenagers. We need to be aware of what they are being exposed to and be willing to step in when they are not yet able to make appropriate decisions for themselves.

So when did we as parents go deaf and blind? We look at the cover of a book our kids bring home from school, the latest CD they want to buy at the store, or newest popular movie they want to see and we say, "Oh, that looks pretty cool." Or maybe we say, "Well, I hear it's not too good, but it has a good story line." Then we let them immerse themselves in it, and we wonder why we see the same type of rebellious, perverted behavior rising up in them.

"Stop being so concerned about being your child's "Buddy" and step into the role of being their parent!"

Parents, be the grown up, say "No" to your children when you need to and then explain to them why. Stop being so concerned about being their "buddy" and step into the role of being their parent. Come on, your child's soul is at stake! A priority of your laboring in God's harvest field is to train them up and send them into their marketplace as a light in a dark world, an encouragement to their peers. Show them that it is good and righteous to stand with God, to declare the name of Jesus Christ!

Demonstrate to them by your example that if you humble yourself under God's mighty hand, He will guide you in making right decisions so you won't spend years of your life regretting what could have easily been avoided. Send your Godly equipped children into the marketplace to encourage their teachers, their employers and their peers to shine the light of Jesus wherever they go.

What about the adults? Bottomline is if you're not doing it, your kids won't do it. You need to be pursuing God, focusing on that which honors Christ and how to better equip yourself to fulfill the CHRISTian's Commission (Matt 28:18-20). First by being the example of Christ to your family, then taking the Gospel to your workplace, treating the employees with integrity and honesty, treating your boss with honor. If you humble yourself in God's eyes. He will position you for providence to proclaim His name and share His message.

Do you wonder why you don't seem to be going in the right direction? Always struggling, never feeling on top of things? Then ask yourself, "Am I laboring for the harvest? Am I joining God in His work? Am I providing for and partnering with my local church? Are lost souls on my mind? And if so how am I reaching them?

I want to encourage you, let today be the day! Seize the moment in the position which you have been placed. You are positioned for providence, for God's divine intervention in your life. Take the step! Make the decision to do something with what you have been given, the position where you are right now. Abandon your self-sufficiency, take on the humility and righteousness of Christ. Become a laborer with the Father and step boldly into the harvest field. Doing this just might put you right smack in the middle of God's provision.

The Bible reveals to us that the time is almost up and we need laborers for the harvest. You have been positioned for providence. What decision will you make to capitalize on this opportunity and step into your destiny? We need God's fresh fire, a renewed baptism in the Holy Spirit. A renewed fervor for prayer and fasting. We need a desperation for God and His Word that exceeds our need for oxygen.

CHRISTian, you must lead the way and repent of your Elimelech ways. You must follow Christ with your whole being! Die to your agenda and be Christ to your world, beginning with your family! You must do whatever is necessary to abandon self-sufficiency and position yourself and your family for the providence of God! It is time!

"…do whatever is necessary to abandon self-sufficiency and position yourself and your family for the providence of God!"

CHAPTER 7

PUTTING FEET TO YOUR FAITH

Ruth returns from the fields and Naomi asks "Where have you been?" So she told Naomi everything that happened. When Ruth reveals the name of the man who had been so kind Naomi must have thrown her hands up with joy, "Praise God! He is taking care of the living and the dead! Boaz is our near kinsman!" Ruth had no idea what she had stumbled onto. Immediately Naomi goes to work instructing Ruth about what to do next. Naomi was carefully positioning Ruth for providence.

Ruth 3:1-5

Then Naomi her mother-in-law said unto her, My daughter, shall I not seek rest for thee? that it may be well with thee? And now is not Boaz of our kindred, with whose maidens thou wast? Behold, he winnoweth barley tonight in the threshing floor. Wash thyself therefore, and anoint thee, and put thy raiment upon thee, and get thee down to the floor: but make not thyself known unto the man, until he shall have done eating and drinking. And it shall be, when he lieth down, that thou shalt mark the place where he shall lie, and thou shalt go in, and uncover his feet, and lay thee down; and he will tell thee what thou shalt do. And she said unto her, All that thou sayest unto me I will do.

It is the responsibility, yet not legal obligation, for the near kinsmen to redeem members of their family who were unable to redeem themselves. Have you ever had overwhelming debts you were unable to pay? Maybe you bought a home, a new car, lots of unnecessary CHRIST-mas presents, purchased all of the newest technology and upgrades, name brand clothes, or several other miscellaneous things we can just call "stuff". Finally you stop and look around to realize that you are on the verge of going under.

Maybe you are one of the rare responsible ones who just can't seem to catch a break. No extra income, no pay raise in sight, no bonuses or unexpected cash flow headed your way to intercept the wave of bills filling your mailbox. Have you ever felt that way before? This is America, the statistics have told on you and me both. Financially we're in a bad way, and it doesn't seem to be getting any better.

Is there a way out? Can I be redeemed? Can I be freed from this burden? This is where the Old Testament kinsmen had the opportunity to step in and save the family. He could pay your debt on your behalf and bring you back to a right standing in the community. Remember though, this was not his legal obligation. He didn't have to do it, it was an option that was offered to him.

"Is there a way out? Can I be redeemed? Can I be freed from this burden?"

Naomi is amazed. God has not only provided necessities, but has brought them to the one who could redeem her family. Even though she was not personally blood related to Boaz, her deceased husband Elimelech was. She knew that through Boaz her family could be redeemed. Naomi begins to share her excitement with Ruth and knows that because of Ruth's faithfulness to her, it's now her turn to take care of Ruth.

According to the last verse of chapter 2, we can estimate that Ruth has been gleaning in Boaz's fields for at least a couple of months. At the end of the season, Naomi instructs Ruth to go back to the threshing floor and wait there until Boaz is through with the end of harvest celebration. She then tells Ruth to find out where he sleeps, and go and sleep at his feet at nightfall. "...mark the place where he shall lie, and that thou shalt go in, and uncover his feet, and lay thee down; and he will tell thee what thou shalt do."

There's a decision on the table. Will Ruth follow the instructions of her mother-in-law or will she decide that she's not up for this challenge? I mean really, think about it. Not the most comfortable of situations, especially if you were rejected. Verse 5, Ruth replies,

"All that thou sayest unto me I will do."

It is one thing to hear counsel from people; it is another thing to heed it. How many times have you had someone ask you, "What do you think?" Maybe they're going to make a big purchase, maybe it's regarding a relationship, or maybe a career change. So since they asked, you tell them what you think. That's when you find out that they really didn't want to know what you think. They actually wanted to hear you say back to them what they wanted to hear. They wanted to hear that their decision was right. They wanted to hear that what they are about to do is not as dumb as it really is. They really don't want to hear your opinion.

Having someone receive counsel and actually apply it is rare, but it's exactly what Ruth did. She didn't know the culture, this was not even her "god", this was Naomi's God. So Naomi took it upon herself to train up Ruth in the traditions of her people, and the ways of her God. Ruth made the decision to put feet to her faith, she decided to obey the counsel of her mother-in-law and committed to do everything she was instructed to do. Verse 6 takes us on Ruth's midnight journey,

> *"...she went down unto the floor, and did according to all that her mother-in-law bade her. And when Boaz had eaten and drunk, and his heart was merry, he went to lie down at the end of the heap of corn: and she came softly, and uncovered his feet, and laid her down. And it came to pass at midnight, that the man was afraid and turned himself: and, behold, a woman lay at his feet. And he said, Who art thou? And she answered, I am Ruth thine handmaid: spread therefore thy skirt over thine handmaid; for thou art a near kinsman."*

This is where we are going to have to pause for a moment. We need to purify our minds of the modern, immoral, American culture. Ruth was not climbing into the sack with Boaz. She was not seducing him or attempting to engage in a sexual relationship.

Ruth was wanting more than the flighty pleasures of the self-serving heart, she wanted a relationship, a life-long covenant-bond with this man. She was seeking redemption. When the Scripture says that she "slept at his feet", it was an act of humility. Her actions were letting him know that she respects him and didn't want to disgrace or dishonor him, but that she is requesting audience with him. Ruth's assignment was to ask Boaz if he would redeem her mother-in-law's family and bring them under his covering, and this was exactly what she did.

She had no rights in this foreign land of Bethlehem-Judah. She was not related to Boaz, only Naomi and that was by marriage. Boaz could have told her, "I have enough troubles around here without the the extra burden of redeeming anybody." But instead he asks who is there?" "It's Ruth, your servant. Take me in and redeem me, for you are my near kinsmen. You alone are where my hope and redemption lies."

In verse 10, Boaz replies,

"Blessed by thou of the Lord, my daughter: for thou has showed more kindness in the later end than at the beginning, inasmuch as thou followedst not young men, whether poor or rich. And now, my daughter, fear not; I will do to thee all that thou requirest: for all the city of my people doth know that thou art a virtuous woman."

Think about the bravery of this young foreigner. Ruth is stepping out strictly on faith, faith that her mother-in-law will not give her bad counsel; faith that Boaz will respond with compassion. I would think she must have been trembling inside.

Various thoughts racing through her mind, all of the "What If?" scenarios. But in fact Boaz responds in a way that shouts of his righteous character. He wakes up, finds Ruth humbly positioned at his feet, hears her request and declares, "I am amazed by you. My whole city knows that you are virtuous!"

Wow! Wouldn't you like people to know that about you? To know about your great reputation even if they don't know you personally. Would you like the members of your community to know that you are a virtuous woman, or a man of integrity? You can, but it's not just going to happen. That kind of press comes when they see how you act and respond in everyday life.

First of all, how you interact with your family, then around your supervisors, your co-workers and your subordinates. You must be consistent in every relationship and situation. When they see how you interact even when no one is watching, that's when you gain the respect of those around you.

The whole city had marked Ruth, a Moabite woman, as virtuous! Boaz says, "You are kinder today than the first day I met you." Imagine what may have been going through his mind, "You could have gone your own way, done your own thing. You could have easily chosen one of my young harvesters to be with and still have been taken care of. After all, they are my trusted men. I will keep them working, I will provide for them. You could have, but you didn't. You found me. You came to me."

Ruth chose God's way rather than her way. Only in God's way is redemption possible, but it does require one thing from you. Redemption requires humility. It is going to take you laying down your pride and everything else you hold dear at the feet of Jesus, letting go and accepting the redemption He has already paid for with His own blood.

"Only in God's way is redemption possible, but it does require one thing of you. Redemption requires humility."

Boaz was a confident man, a business owner, a real man's man, probably an older gentleman who had the esteem and respect of the community. I believe he was amazed that Ruth chose God's way rather than her own. He was so enamored by her faith that he assured her, he would do everything she requested of him.

Being such a righteous man he had to tell her that, in fact, he was not the kinsman that would be next in line to redeem her and this individual must be given first opportunity. So he instructs her to wait there and he will approach the nearer kinsmen to see if he is willing to fulfill his role as the redeemer. Then he comforts her by telling her that if that person refuses then he will, without hesitation, assume the role of kinsman redeemer to her and Naomi.

Once again this shows the integrity of this righteous man. Knowing the responsibility of the redeemer, Boaz also understands that if he does takes Ruth as his wife, his first-born son is given the name of Ruth's dead husband,

Naomi's son. This act of selflessness redeems Elimelech's bloodline and reestablishes it to its former position of inheritance.

It's amazing as shared by Apostle Paul in Romans chapter 11, how God takes people from the wild olive tree, the Gentiles, and grafts them into the natural olive tree, the Jewish nation, making them one. A Moabite woman, who is not only a foreigner, but not even blood related to the lineage is now in line to be redeemed by a member of her late father-in-law's family. Because of God's grace and the obedience of a Jewish man, Elimelech's family is not only re-established, but inevitably included in the bloodline of Christ Himself!

So Ruth, a Moabite, ends up being King David's grandmother. Only God can orchestrate such a plan and perform such glorious redemption out of such tragedy. This is the redemptive power of God. That is the way our God operates. What Boaz does next is equally as astounding. In 3:15-18 Boaz tells Ruth,

"Bring the veil that thou hast upon thee, and hold it. And when she held it, he measured six measures of barley, and laid it on her: and she went into the city. And when she came to her mother-in-law, she said, Who art thou, my daughter? (Meaning how did things work out for you?) And she told her all that the man had done to her. And she said, These six measures of barley gave he me; for he said to me, Go not empty unto thy mother-in-law. Then said she, Sit still, my daughter, until thou know how the matter will fall: for the man will not be in rest, until he has finished the thing this day."

Boaz arises early to insure Ruth can be home before sunrise so her reputation is not marred by being seen together. He then pulls out six measures of the grain he had just finished harvesting and he puts it in Ruth's apron and tells her to take it to her mother-in-law. When Naomi sees the grain, she exclaims, "What is this?" You can sense the excitement in her voice, it's because she recognized the sign of a covenant. Naomi saw this as Boaz' way of telling her "I will make sure you are taken care of one way or another. Your redemption draweth nigh."

"Your redemption draweth nigh."

Six measures of grain, this gesture translated to Naomi and Ruth that there was genuine hope of redemption. This amount of grain would equate to around 40 pounds worth. Six measures out of Boaz' abundance may have seemed like nothing to him, yet to Naomi it was everything. To her it meant "identity restored, life preserved, inheritance established".

Let's think, for a moment, about how God looks at this. You were separated from God by your sinful actions and decisions. You had turned your back on Him and were considered a foreigner to His blessing. God declares His intention to redeem you, even though you choose to continue living in sin, and sends His Son Jesus Christ to pay the price of your redemption with His own blood shed on the Cross. God, the Father, has for you an abundant fulness of blessings beyond your understanding, beginning with your salvation.

Once you realize that you are the one who Christ died to redeem, you repent of your sin and turn toward Him. Then

God applies the fulness of the paid price of Christ's blood. He removes all of your sin and pays all of your debt. As soon as you trust in Him, He gives you an interest on that payment called the Holy Spirit. At that moment you have been reconciled to God, brought back into a right standing with Him once again. This is referred to in Greek as "Eirene", to set at one again, a full restoration.

Too many times we forget that the Father's intent was for Jesus Christ to be the door to the Throne-room. The access to stand in His presence and worship Him in confidence. When we see what God did for us through Jesus Christ, we should realize that the abundance of Christ is waiting for us if we just trust in Him.

When Naomi saw Ruth with the portion of grain Boaz had given to her, she knew that this was only a token of what he would make available to her after he performed his redemptive work.

Please understand this is not a "Gimmee Gimick", we're not coming to God for Him to be at our beckon call and meet all of our requests. We are coming to God because we are sinners who have offended Him by our actions and we realize that He is the only one who can redeem us back into the realm of the spiritual living, rather than continuing as a member of the spiritually dead.

This abundance of blessing is the fulness of His Spirit that we now have access to through Christ. The pinnacle of our salvation is not about what we gain here on earth, but that we have been made right with God and will be with Him in eternity.

In John 14:6, Jesus says to His disciple, "I am the way, the truth and the life. No man comes to the Father but by

Me." Only through Jesus are the blessings of God available, and those blessings are beyond your comprehension. These are not blessings to heap upon yourself so that you might feel better, or even more comfortable. These are blessings to greater prepare you to do His work. You must prepare! In James 1:17 we are encouraged to know that God will provide for you, that all good and perfect gifts come from our heavenly Father. But your vision must not be consumed with "What can God do for me?" Instead, you should be focused on "What can I do for God?". The Father desires that none should be lost. If you are a true child of God, your focus should always recalibrate back to His vision, being His witness and declaring His Gospel message. To bring the redemptive power of God to the world who are lost and without Christ.

We live in a high tech, fast-paced, multi-tasking world, filled with the touted "Mosaic Thinkers", which is really just another way of saying, "I can do a lot of things at once, but none of them very well".

Even with all of our electronic smart devices, we actually lose track of time more often now than when we were dependent on a wrist watch and pocket calendar. The demands on our time and our psyche are at an all time high and don't appear to be slowing down anytime soon. It is for this reason we must decide to slow down a little and give our life to Him who matters most. We must return to the place where Jesus Christ is preeminent. We must be responsible to take the necessary action to afford us the time to refocus, that which puts us on our knees in the presence of our Father. Revelation 2:4 "…thou hast left the first love."

"...thou hast left the first love."

All the technological advances have been developed and sold to us as devices that would allow us to be more productive, more organized and more in control of our time. You would naturally think that you will have more time to read God's Word; more time to pray and worship; more time to help someone in need; time to encourage someone or even meet someone for coffee to share what God is doing in your life. In fact this is exactly the opposite of what has happened.

We are loosely connected with more people today than ever before. In 2014, the over 1.3 million FaceBook users in the United States posted almost 400,000 "Likes" per minute. The average FaceBook user between the ages of 18-24 has upwards of 650 friends (According to www.statista.com) and that's only one social network! According to www.pewinternet.org over 74% of Internet users are engaged in social networking. You do the math. It boggles my mind how we can be loosely engaged in so many relationships and think everything is good. yet at the same time our marriages are falling apart and our children are losing touch with the stability of God's design for "family".

As you read the Bible, pray for the Holy Spirit to give you personal revelation, receive the counsel of Godly people, and then you can stand on God's promises with confidence. I am not going back to some heretical doctrine that says we have to hold God to his Word. God does not have to be held to his Word.

He knows his Word very well. He hasn't forgotten it, nor does He have to be reminded. It is me! I am the one that needs to be held to His Word. I am the one who needs to be reminded that God is faithful. I am the one who must rid myself of this selfish mindset and be clothed in the mind of Christ (1 Corinthians 2:16).

CHAPTER 8

SIT STILL

Ruth 3:18

Then she (Naomi) said, Sit still, my daughter, until thou know how the matter will fall: for the man will not be in rest, until he have finished the thing this day.

At first, Ruth didn't know anything about Naomi's God except that He had proven himself faithful to preserve them and provide for them over the last few months. Unlike most of us, Ruth actually listened to and followed her mother-in-law's counsel. She requested of Boaz the redemption that was promised. Now Naomi is now telling her to wait patiently because their redemption is in process.

Ruth 4:1

Then went Boaz up to the gate, and sat him down there: and, behold, the kinsman of whom Boaz spake came by;

unto whom he said, Ho, such a one! turn aside, sit down here. And he turned aside, and sat down. And he took ten men of the elders of the city, and said, Sit ye down here. And they sat down. And he said unto the kinsman, Naomi, that is come again out of the country of Moab, selleth a parcel of land, which was our brother Elimelech's: And I thought to advertise thee, saying, Buy it before the inhabitants, and before the elder's of my people. If thou wilt redeem it, redeem it: but if thou wilt not redeem it, then tell me, that I may know: for there is none to redeem it besides thee; and I am after thee. And he said, I will redeem it.

Let's stop here for just a minute and remember how they got here. So many times God takes us back to where He wants us to be? Willing or not, we find ourselves returning to the point of decision where we were years ago, a second chance to see if we are willing to listen to Him this time. Surely this is undeniable evidence of God's grace.

The story of Ruth is all about decisions. Elimelech made a decision. His decision to follow man's solution rather than abide in God's provision almost removed his family out of the line of inheritance, and out of the lineage of Israel except for the grace of God. The effect of this decision took both he and his family out from under God's provision and led them into a foreign land, the land of man's solution.

Naomi also made a decision. Her decision brought her back to her homeland. She knew there was no other place she could go for blessing other than the land of God's provision. Then following her mother in-law's example Ruth made her decision as well. She decided to selflessly accompany Naomi on her journey.

It's of importance to note that Ruth did not just stand and wait for something to happen. She didn't wait for an invitation from Naomi, she knew what was in her heart to do and she stepped out in faith to pursue it.

Elimelech was driven by circumstance. Naomi was driven by necessity. Ruth was driven by humility.

Are you at that point, right now, today? Are you being driven by circumstance or by necessity? Do you keep thinking you are going to find God's provision somewhere else?

"Surely God can't be so narrow-minded that there is only one road back to Him." "Surely God sees where I am, He knows my heart and He understands why I have not fully committed to Him, right?" "Surely He's not going to judge me just because I'm not perfect. I mean who is?" "I mean God understands why I still hold on to my addictions, my bad behaviors, my selfishness, rebellion, un-forgiveness, etc., right?"

Yes God does understand. He is God, and because He is God He will not compromise His standard or the way we can access Him. To do so would betray His proclaimed love for us, nullify His Deity, and defile HIs righteousness. To compromise His Holy standard would contradict His character and make Him a liar. But we know that it is impossible for God to lie (Titus 1:2). We can trust God to be who He says He is and do what He says He will do.

"Are you driven by circumstance or by necessity?"

So the truth remains, God's blessing is only found in the land of His provision, and there is only one way to receive it, through the Cross. If you're driven by circumstance, you will find yourself in a different place every time you roll out of bed. Circumstance will never keep you at the Cross. It might lead you there, but it will change in the next moment leading you to another rabbit trail and taking you further from what you truly desire.

Necessity must be your driver. The necessity to be where God is and will land you at the foot of the cross in desperation. It's when you see yourself for who you really are, a soul lost in your sin, destined for destruction, you become desperate. You realize that in fact there is only one way to the Father and it is through Jesus Christ.

But it is in humility that you truly acknowledge your unworthiness to receive such a gift and in desperation you cry out to God, reaching for His salvation only to find that He's been waiting arms open, face gleaming, ready to receive you all along. Humility allows you to stay in His presence, and when you are there you will not want to be anywhere else. At that moment you are safe, you are accepted and you are loved. God is gracious and He will visit you outside of His provision, but He is not going to live there with you. He wants to provoke you to a place of necessity, a burning desire to be clothed in His Spirit and a humility to receive His gracious gift.

All it takes is one decision. Naomi made her decision to return and because she did Ruth made the decision to follow. Ruth chose to deny everything, her past, her community, her traditions, everything familiar in order to embrace her mother-in-law and trust in her decision, "Your people will now be my people and your God will now be my God.".

Let's allow God to prove himself as the God of provision. Ruth didn't just make a decision to follow Naomi, she made a decision to provide for her. She made a decision to listen to and follow her mother-in-law's counsel.

The power of decision. The results of what we've been discussing were based on one decision, one at a time. What if you could see your life's decisions graphed out on a chart? Every time you made a decision a little dot appeared on the lifeline of your graph. Each dot connected to the previous dot as each decision was made. Not just the big decisions, but every decision.

We tend to place our primary focus on the big decisions when in reality each decision provides adjustments, whether minor or major to your course direction.

Every decision that we make now affects something or someone. Somewhere in the future, somewhere in the lives of others, your decisions are charting a course to a destination and affecting others along the way. Our decisions have a compound effect.

One little stone pebble tossed into the water will ripple across the whole lake. You can see its effects only so far, but the molecules are still moving, most likely until the the ripple hits the shore. You never know how far the impact of your decision will reach, but God knows.

"Our decisions have a compound affect."

As you review the decision-dots on your lifeline, you start making some observations noticing a few little bumps, upward and downward.

Hopefully you were blessed as a child to have a strong support system in place, like a loving mom and dad who weren't afraid to provide you with balanced correction and discipline. If this was the case, they helped you to better understand the rewards and consequences of your decisions. So maybe the next time you were faced with a similar situation, you were equipped to make a better decision.

Each decision you made continued to chart the course of your life. It doesn't just effect the moment, it may impact the rest of your life. The decision of whether or not to cheat on your homework in grade school, will be the launching pad for your decision to cheat on you final exams in college. The decision to steal from the company you work for, may be the crack in your integrity that tempts you to be unfaithful to your wife.

The happiest and/or saddest moments of your life will come when you are watching your grandchildren as they reap the consequences, whether positive or negative, of the actions that you passed down to them through your children. One decision will change the course of your life and the lives of others, just one.

If not carefully navigated, you may look back on your life-graph and see something that looks more like an EKG of a heart-attack victim whose heart is spiraling out of control. But it doesn't have to be that way. Today is the day that you can turn it all around. Your life-graph has the potential to reveal a steady upward trend of learning and growing. Whether you feel your life is in continuous downturn or a steady upward trend, it's at that moment you realize it is only by God's grace that you are here today reading this book.

The greatest thing about it all is that God provides opportunity for correction and growth in the midst of each failure, if we will only humble ourselves, repent and refocus on Him. God's forgiveness will clean our slate, but it doesn't mean all of the consequences just disappear. Yes, there is still an effect, but He is there to help us get through it.

I once heard a story about a little boy who would get furiously angry at the drop of a hat. He would throw himself on the ground, call people names, even punch and kick anyone who got in his way. After one of these episodes his dad said, "Son, here is a box of nails. Do you see our beautiful redwood fence over there? You know, the one that you helped me build last summer?" The boy said, "Yeah dad, I see it." The father continued, "Every time you get mad and want to throw a fit, I want you to take this hammer and this box of nails and pound a nail into that fence as hard as you can." So the boy did just as his dad told him. For the next week every time he felt the urge to throw a fit he would grab the hammer and a hand full of nails and start pounding away!

Wham, wham, wham! The neighbors thought he was using a nail gun he was so intense. He didn't hold anything back, after all his dad gave him permission.

By the end of the week he had finally went through the entire box of nails. His dad came to his son and said, "So you finished the nails?" "Yep!" said the boy, "I went through the whole box dad, and I feel so much better!" "Great!" the dad said, "Now I want you to take out all of the nails that you drove in." "Whaaat!" the boy exclaimed. "Go remove every single nail you hammered into our beautiful redwood fence." Not happy, at all, his son spent the next three days pulling, pounding and bending every last one of the nails out of the fence.

At the end of the third day, after removing the last nail, the boy sat down. Exhausted, tired and not feeling too well, his father came over and sat beside him. "Son, I want you to step back and take a look at our beautiful redwood fence. The fence that you and I worked so hard to make perfect."

The boy steps back, his eyes widened while his jaw dropped. "What do you see son?" The boy replied, "I see ugliness dad. I see holes, chunks of the fence actually busted and laying on the ground. I see splintered boards where our beautiful fence once stood." As he spoke tears began to well up in his eyes. He looked at his dad through his tears and said, "I'm so sorry dad. Please forgive me!" "You see son," said the dad, "even though you removed all of the nails, the damage made while you were pounding them in and then pulling them back out again have left our beautiful fence broken, fractured and in complete disarray. Regardless how careful you try to be, the wood is never the same." "It looks horrible dad, I can't believe I did that!" said the son.

"That's the lesson son. Just like decisions you make in your life. Once you make them, that nail has been driven into the fabric of your life and the lives of all those you affect. Thankfully God will give you a chance to pull that nail out, but there will always be an effect left behind." "But dad, what about forgiveness?" "I do forgive you son, I love you, but that doesn't fix the fence. This is where God's mercy and grace comes in son. Only He can give you the power to forgive and be forgiven. But you must have a humble heart to receive His gift, then the healing can begin."

"...every decision you make impacts the course of your life and the lives of many, many others."

At one point in your life, you realize every decision you make impacts the course of your life and the lives of many, many others. Elimelech's decision took his family to the Land of Man's Solution and endangered his lineage. Naomi's decision to return to the Land of God's Provision aligned them for restoration. Ruth's decision positioned them for the fulfilling of God's Providence.

When Naomi receives from Ruth the six measures of barley that Boaz had sent to her, she sees more than just the barley, she sees hope, even the possibility of redemption. Once Naomi hears of Boaz' message to her, she tells Ruth to wait patiently. Namoi knew that Boaz wouldn't rest until he had taken care of this matter. Boaz realized there was one who was a closer kinsman than he was and knew he needed to follow the proper steps to insure Naomi's redemption.

What's the hardest thing you've ever done when you're not in control? When your life weighs in the balance, your livelihood is at stake, and it all rests in the hands of someone else? WAIT! Yep, the simplicity of waiting becomes the ultimate form of torture!

Ruth could have ran down to the city gate to see what was happening, but instead she made another decision, the decision to obey. She came to terms with the fact that she could not redeem herself and her redemption was completely in the hands of someone else. The work of redemption can only be done by the Redeemer.

Do we truly understand this? You cannot redeem yourself. The completion of the redemptive work in your life can only be done by your Redeemer. So she waits. And Boaz did just as he said, he went straight to the gate the next morning. Watching intently, he was not going to miss this near-kinsmen/redeemer.

There he was nearing the gate, Boaz shouts out, "Hey, come on over here!" Boaz explains to him the details of the situation and that it's his responsibility to redeem Naomi if he chooses to do so. Then Boaz lays out the conditions; the kinsman must buy back the land from Naomi in order to restore her family back into the lineage. And he says, okay, I guess I can do that.

"The work of redemption can only be done by the Redeemer."

Boaz exemplifies integrity in this scene. He goes to the city gate, addresses the issue with the near-kinsman, and never attempts to manipulate the outcome. He gives this man an honest chance to redeem Naomi's family line to which he accepts, well at least for a moment. Then Boaz tells him that there is a little bit more to it. In chapter 4, verse 5:

Then said Boaz, What day thou buyest the field of the hand of Naomi, thou must buy it also of Ruth the Moabitess, the wife of the dead, to raise up the name of the dead upon his inheritance.

He just gave him the fine print. It is not just about a piece of land here my brother. Not only do you have to redeem Naomi, but you have to redeem Ruth who was the widow of your relative which means you will be responsible to raise up his family name through a son you will have with her. At that point the kinsman said, "I'm out!". Verse 6:

And the kinsman said, I cannot redeem it for myself, lest I mar mine own inheritance: redeem thou my right to thyself; for I cannot redeem it.

It was the custom in Israel that to confirm all things regarding redeeming and making changes that the man was required to take off his shoe and give it to his neighbor as a testimony to his people. Verse 7 continues:

Therefore the kinsman said unto Boaz, Buy it for thee. So he drew off his shoe. And Boaz said unto the elders, and unto the people, Ye are witnesses this day, that I have bought all that was Elimelech's, and all that was Chilion's and Mahlon's, of the hand of Naomi. Moreover, Ruth the Moabitess, the wife of Mahlon, have I purchased to be my wife, to raise up the name of the dead upon his inheritance, that the name of the dead be not cut off from among his brethren, and from the gate of his place: ye are witnesses this day.

At this time Boaz could have hesitated. He could have taken this opportunity to back out and think about his decision. "What is this going to cost me, having to take care of a wife and family? My first born son will have to be the namesake of Ruth's deceased husband. He won't even have my name. Do I really have time for this? I mean, I'm a successful businessman! Not only that, but Ruth is a foreigner. I've lived here all my life and have a good reputation. Everyone knows I follow God's commandments. What will they say if I marry a women who is not an Israelite? I could come under persecution or ridicule. Maybe this isn't such a good idea. Maybe I need to think about this a little harder."

How many times have we used the old excuse, "Let me pray about it for a while." Just think about what would happen if we actually prayed before we made decisions. Then when the time came to make a decision we would more than likely already have the answer. Instead, we panic because we haven't been in prayer and in turn miss the opportunity to achieve the greatest impact.

This does not mean we are to make snap decisions and not take time to pray. It only means that too many times we aren't prepared, so by the time we get back from our "time of prayer" the impact of that opportunity is gone.

But not Boaz. He had obviously already prayed about this and was ready to follow the doors God opened. Boaz had been watching Ruth during the time that she was working with his servants. It could be that Boaz was even wondering when this day would come since it was the widow's obligation to request for the redemptive process to be enacted.

Boaz had no obligation to oblige this request. Could it be that maybe the morning he woke up and found Ruth at his feet on the floor that he had already been in prayer for God's direction? It only stands to reason. When the time came for him to make the final decision, he didn't hesitate.

When the nearest kinsman refused to redeem Naomi's family, Boaz immediately accepted the responsibility with a confident., "I will redeem them.".

How many times do we put our faith in redeemers that have no desire to redeem us? We put our hope in things, in careers, and in relationships. We put our hope in stuff rather than in God. In the end all of these faux-redeemers will end up responding, "I can't do it. I can't bear that extra load. I can't take on your burden." When you set your sights on anyone or anything but Christ, you are setting yourself up only to be let down again. Christ alone is our Redeemer.

"How many times do we put our faith in redeemers that have no desire to redeem us?"

Verse 11 says:

> *"And all the people that were in the gate, and the elders, said, We are witnesses. The Lord make the woman that is come into thine house like Rachel and like Leah, which too did built the house of Israel: and do thou worthily in Ephratah, and be famous in Bethlehem: And let thy house be like the house of Pharez, whom Tamar bear unto Judah of the seed which the Lord shall given thee of this young woman. So Boaz took Ruth,"*

Let's think about this for a second. Naomi's family had dwelt in Moab for ten years. We do not know if they arrived there and the sons immediately found and married wives because scripture doesn't say. What we do know is that Elimelech and his family arrived there, his sons found wives and they dwelt there for ten years.

So regardless of how long Ruth was married to Mahlon they had no children, no heirs to whom they could pass the inheritance to. A child with Boaz would be a first for both of them, yet it would have to be placed under Mahlon's heritage.

This detail did not seem to discourage Boaz from his decision one bit. Not only did Boaz solidify the covenant with the kinsman among several witnesses, he immediately took Ruth to be his wife and consummated his relationship with her in order to fulfill the remainder of his covenant obligation.

Verse 13 tells us that Boaz slept with his new wife and "...the Lord gave her conception, and she bear a son."

CHAPTER 9
LINEAGE RESTORED

Isn't it interesting, she was unable to conceive with Mahlon, yet it appears almost immediately after marrying Boaz she was able to conceive? Coincidence, I don't think so. It was the effect of Ruth's decision to return with Naomi and Boaz's decision to accept the role of kinsman/redeemer. At that one moment, Elimelech's family line was redeemed back into the land of God's provision through a child conceived by Boaz and Ruth.

Chapter 4, verse 14:

"And the women said unto Naomi, Blessed be the Lord, which hath not left thee this day without a kinsman, that his name may be famous in Israel. And he shall be unto thee a restorer of thy life, and a nourisher of thine old age: for thy daughter-in-law, which loveth thee, which is better to thee than seven sons, hath born him. And Naomi took the child, and laid it in her bosom, and became nurse unto it."

Wow! The whole community recognized the hand of God working on Naomi's behalf. All the women of the village were so excited that they were coming out to pray blessings on the new baby. The elders of the city came and prayed blessings on Boaz and his new family.

None of the things that could have come against Boaz for taking this risk happened. He was not persecuted by his peers for marrying a foreign woman. He did not lose his reputation as a businessman or elder in the community. In fact, the city rejoiced because they recognized the Hand of God restoring Elimelech's family back into the lineage. The women were the ones who even named the child and acknowledged Ruth's value to the family when they said, "Ruth has been better to you than seven sons."

Read Ruth 4:9-22.

"Ruth has been better to you than seven sons."

You see, at that time having a son was a blessing. The son was to provide for you in your old age. To have a good, responsible son was a very good thing. You felt a security in your future. But to have "seven sons" would have been the epitome of a perfect blessing. The women told Naomi that Ruth was better to her than "seven sons".

Why would they say that? If Naomi would have had seven sons, they would have had seven wives, seven families and only God knows how many kids each would have had. Each one distracted by all of life's turmoil, just trying to get by squeezing you in around everything else.

But Ruth's total focus and attention was to redeem Naomi's house. Think about it. She didn't say, "Oh Naomi,

I am going to go with you just to see what I can get out of this whole thing." No, the first thing she did was to provide for Naomi by going out and gleaning in the fields. She was not raised in Israel; she didn't know the customs of kinsman/redeemer; she only knew she needed to care for her mother-in-law. Ruth's entire purpose was to provide for her mother-in-law and see to it that she was properly cared for in her old age.

God honored Ruth's dedication and not only insured Naomi was restored back into the lineage of Israel, but gave Ruth a husband, a family, a home and even a place in the lineage of Christ.Verse 16 is so incredible to me. It says,

> *"Naomi took Ruth and Boaz's child and laid it in her bosom and became nurse unto it."*

Naomi was now a grandma, the first time! She had the privilege of being in her homeland and providing love and security to her new grandson. When Naomi came back to Bethlehem she told the community, "Don't call me Naomi anymore, instead call me Mara, because I am bitter and God has frowned on me."

What a sharp contrast as she now gazes into the face of her beautiful grandson and looks across the room at her loving daughter-in-law and her husband as they smile watching grandma hold their son, knowing that this was all possible because of God's redeeming grace and the decisions of those He had placed around her who were willing to reach for and obtain the redemption that had been provided for her.

I see Naomi like she has never been before. She knows God has smiled on her. She knows that she is loved, favored by God beyond her dreams. The little baby lying in her arms represented the fulfillment of her redemption. Every time she looked at her grandson, she remembers – "God loves me." God honored my dead husband and my dead sons and brought us back into a right standing with God's people. This baby is the proof. He is the evidence of God's provision.

What a joyous thing! Just think about it as a born again child of God. Every time you look into the mirror you can say, "I am the evidence of the love God has for me. I am the evidence that God desires to redeem me, to save me from my sins. Every time you look in the mirror, don't just see yourself, you see the person Christ died for. Think about that baby that was born in a manger, the manifested presence of God's deliverance for his people, delivered to all of humanity. He restored us, He completed us, and now we look into the mirror and see the recipient of all He has done.

Naomi's neighbors, fellow women in the village, rejoiced with Naomi. In verse 17,

> *"And the women her neighbors gave it a name, saying, There is a son born to Naomi; and they called his name Obed:"*

So who gave the baby his name? It's mother, or grandmother? Nope, the group of women who were celebrating God's honor upon Naomi. These women had seen the wonderful, graciousness of God's hand.

They had watched as Ruth and Naomi walked back into the city. They whispered and they wondered. They saw Naomi overcome with bitterness. They saw the young Moabite woman with her, completely out of place, yet walking arm in arm. "What is going to happen?", they must have asked each other. "What will become of Naomi? What will her end be?" But this day, they celebrated and rejoiced as they declared the name of the new baby, "We are going to name him Obed!"

The miracles never stop. When we yield to God's Providence, we position ourselves to be recipients of His provision. Look at the incredible blessing that is revealed in chapter 4:18-22.

"Now these are the generations of Pharez: Pharez begat Hezron, And Hezron begat Ram, and Ram begat Amminadab, Amminadab begat Nahshon, Nahshon begat Salmon, And Salmon begat Boaz, and Boaz begat Obed, And Obed begat Jesse, and Jesse begat David."

"...and they called his name Obed."

Obed? Definitely not a common name, not even in the Bible. What does Obed mean? The name Obed means servant worshiper, or a servant who worships, a worshiper of the most high God. Those ladies of the city gave that child a name that would remind his family of God's redemption and deliverance. None of them had the slightest clue that they had been placed into the lineage of the Messiah Himself. Obed had no idea that he would become the grandfather of king David, the greatest King Israel ever had.

There's another reason this is so exciting. Ruth was a foreigner. She was a Gentile, just like me and possibly just like you. As a godless Gentile, Ruth had no part of Israel's inheritance. Yet God takes a woman from a foreign land called Moab, the place of man's solutions, and because of her obedience and the decisions that she makes to follow Him, He integrates this Gentile who would traditionally pollute the Jewish bloodline into the lineage of Christ. By doing this God sends young Ruth a very special message. "I have not forgotten the Gentile nation because I have provided redemption for you also."

The Bible says that we denied even the very knowledge and existence of God. We fought against God. We fought against God's people. We represent everything that was not God. Yet He extends HIs grace. Acts 28:28

> *"Be it known therefore unto you, that the salvation of God is sent unto the Gentiles…"*

This is incredible! Boaz went through the proper process of finding the nearest kinsman so that he would be in a right standing when he performed the duties of the redeemer.

You see, our nearest kinsman would have been Adam, but he could not redeem us. The Bible says there had to come a second Adam. Now, think about this very carefully. God, as God, could not redeem us. If He could have, why didn't He just reach down and touch Adam and say, you are redeemed. Why didn't he just reach down and talk to Abel or Seth and say, "Your daddy messed it up, but "Poof!" now you are redeemed and everything is back to normal.

God was a friend with Abraham, so why didn't He just talk to Abraham. Why didn't He just go to Abraham and say, "Abraham, I am going to redeem you. Everybody has messed up before you but you are a good guy and you are my friend so "Poof!" now you are redeemed.

"Even God himself could not redeem us in his current form."

But God, who is Spirit (John 4:24), could not be our redeemer. According to the bloodline, God was not our nearest of kin. Adam was. Even though we were made in the likeness of God, we were not God's kin. We were made in the likeness of God, but we were not God. We are human. We are flesh. We are bone. We are blood. We are tangible. We are temporal.

Our redemption had to come from one who is like us, yet unblemished by sin. But, because God's heart is to redeem His creation and reconcile us back to Himself, He chose to take on the form of man to come to earth and be integrated into the human race. By doing this, God in the form of Jesus Christ became our nearest of kin and because of this and Adam's inability to redeem us, Christ could step in and fulfill the role of our kinsman/redeemer.

Even God Himself could not redeem us in His current form. He had to take on the form of a man, of a human being filled with the power of the Holy Spirit to come in our likeness to be woven into our society, woven into the lineage of the human race, woven in by the decision made by a young Moabitess named Ruth so He could be our near kinsman and provide the redemption that only He could.

Wow! God planned our redemption from the beginning. The Bible says He began this process as soon as Adam and Eve fell. Genesis 3:15 scripture says,

"And I will put enmity between thee and the woman, and between thy seed and her seed; it shall bruise thy head, and thou shalt bruise his heel."

You may ask, "Then why did God wait to show up thousands of years later in the form of Jesus? What took Him so long?" In actuality, God was here the whole time. His Spirit was escorting us to the place of divine providence, preparing us to receive his long awaited redemption.

The following understanding is crucial. Knowing that every decision you make will either positively or negatively affect your future makes it is imperative that you stop making bad ones. I know it seems I'm stating the obvious, but if you're like me still feeling the sting of past decisions gone wrong, then keep reading and we'll get through this together.

Think about this very, very carefully. Ruth's redemption did not come to complete fruition until after what? Not until after Ruth and Boaz had 'labored together'. In thinking about the seasons of the harvest, it appears that between the barley and the time of wheat harvest, Boaz and Ruth would have actually worked together for about three and a half months. During this time, Boaz watched Ruth glean in His fields and it wasn't until after the harvest that her redemption came to completion.

It wasn't until 'after' the harvest, 'after' the labor, 'after' the work was done that the redemption was completed. Ruth had not only proven herself faithful, she had proven herself fruitful. People can be faithful, but it's what or who you are faithful to that makes the difference of whether or not you're fruitful. There are those who are faithful at having only the desire to please themselves and wonder why they are not fruitful and productive in the eternal things of God's Kingdom.

Sadly there are a lot of people in the church that do the exact same thing. We have accepted 'Vogue Christianity' as the norm and complacency as its vehicle. Then we wonder why we don't experience an overcoming life.

We tout ourselves as being Christians, yet we sit in the pew every week without doing anything. No desire to witness to the unsaved, no desire to testify about God's faithfulness, and definitely too busy to lift a finger to help in any ministry capacity as we rush out the doors after service. Why? Because we are driven to meet our needs, our desires, our aspirations. We are our biggest and most important concern.

The true Christian must be faithful 'and' fruitful. Boaz saw Ruth's faithfulness in her labor. But it wasn't until after they had co-labored together in the harvest that her fruitfulness was revealed and the redemption was fulfilled. Your redemption is not totally complete either.

The Bible says that we are still waiting for the completeness of our redemption. Romans 8:22-23,

> *"For we know that the whole creation groaneth and travaileth in pain together until now. And not only they, but ourselves also, which have the firstfruits of the Spirit, even we ourselves groan within ourselves, waiting for the adoption, to wit, the redemption of our body."*

So did Christ leave something out? Is the redemptive work unfinished? Absolutely not! The price has been paid in full by Christ's sacrifice, but we have not cashed in on its fulness because you and I are still here on planet earth, we are still in the midst of the harvest. We cannot expect for our redemption to be complete until we have embraced arms with Christ and labored with Him in the fields. If you have trusted in Christ for your redemption then you are His ambassador to a lost world. The Spirit of the Redeemer lives in you and you are a vessel of that redemption.

If we are not laboring, if we are not working in the harvest field, then we have no right to request redemption. Are we totally encompassed in what God wants us to do? Have we made the harvest our focus? Or are we still so bent on heaping things upon ourselves with us being the focus?

We say we have no time to do what God has commissioned us to do, but we have plenty of time to rebel against Him. We can't find the time to study God's Holy Word, as we run to the kitchen for a snack between episodes of our binge television series. We want to hear His voice, but we can't squeeze Him in around our social media posts, friend requests, or virtual reality games.

Daily we make decisions that counter God's will, saying that God understands because we're only human. Oh yes, He does understand. He understands He has given us a clear directive, that He paid the ultimate price for your Salvation, and that He wants to co-labor with you to reconcile the world back to Himself. When the harvest is over, the completion of our redemption draws nigh. You and I must be about the Father's business.

There is nothing evil about technology. But what are you using it for? What made it evil? Why we did, of course. Why is pornography so hot on the Internet? Because of people.

Why do people steal and kill? Why do we have drugs and addiction? Because of the fallen nature of people. Why do things get abused and neglected? Why do we always go into extremes about things? Because we are human. Why do certain doctrines that come into church start out balanced then become a total overthrow of the doctrine of Christ? Because we are fallen.

"We must get back to the simplicity of the gospel."

We must get back to the simplicity of the gospel, which is found right smack dab in the middle of Boaz' field. It is called harvest. Your redeemer wants to embrace you, but he also wants to work with you.

I am blessed to be the husband of an incredible woman. When I hold Belinda's hand, it is not like I am holding the hand of just anyone. I am holding the hand of someone who has proven herself faithful to me since 1982. I am holding the hand of someone who not only loves me, but knows me and still loves me. I am holding the hand of someone who has co-labored with me all of my adult life, someone who had went through he fire with me and has made me a better person because of who she is. I am holding the hand of someone who has chosen to follow God rather than man. To this day when I look at her, I still get excited and feel the butterflies in my stomach. My heart is overwhelmed with love for her because I know her and she knows me.

This type of relationship comes only by laboring together. The moment we said "I do", our journey began. Jesus wants you to say "I do" to a relationship with Him. He wants you to labor with Him so when tribulation comes you will be able to trust Him to hold you regardless what life brings. He wants you to be as excited about laboring with Him as He is about laboring with you. He desires for you to be one who is willing to surrender all for His purposes and for His cause, no longer consumed by your self serving agenda, but focused with Him on the harvest.

"9-11 was a decision."

Things are changing in America. Nothing has been the same since September 11, 2001. No single event in modern history has affected the world as the tragedy of what will forever be known as simply, 9-11. But 9-11 was a decision. One single decision that began a chain of decisions that for a moment stopped the heartbeat of the world as we stared at our televisions and computer monitors in horror and disbelief.

Things will never be the same because one person made a decision. Osama bin Laden made a decision. He made the decision to reign terror on America and those who followed made their decision to carry out his demonically inspired plan. Thousands upon thousands of lives were affected, not just in the U.S., but all over the world. There aren't many who will read this book that can say this event did not touch them in some personal way.

Immediately following the 9-11 tragedy and for several months following, people were open to hearing the Gospel of Jesus Christ again. Church attendance was up by 25% nationwide. Both the nominal church attender and the non-religious were desiring to be comforted and a sense of stability that they intuitively can only come through a pursuit of God, which they translated as religion. Their hearts were open, they were looking for hope.

School bus drivers began to pray on their routes with the kids with a boldness that the Body of Christ hadn't seen for decades. Teachers began to allow Christian prayer in their classrooms. George W. Bush, the President of the United States at the time, returned to the practice of holding staff prayer meetings in the Oval Office.

Sadly, we learn to adapt and slowly grow numb to the memories. We tout the phrase, "We will never forget", really? Less than a year had passed and the status quo dropped lower than it had been before that horrific event. We need to be ready to go through the open door of people's hearts while we still can.

Tell them about the gospel of Jesus Christ. Tell them about God's love for them. Tell them that God sent his only begotten Son to earth as a little baby born in a stable, wrapped in swaddling clothes and placed in a feeding trough. Tell them that He gave His life to save us from the penalty of our sin and redeem us back to Himself. God loves you and because of HIs great love it's our responsibility to tell the people of this world that He loves them too. Let's join the Father in the harvest.

CHAPTER 10

THE LENGTHS OF REDEMPTION

L et's take a brief snapshot of the miracle of God's mercy: Miracle: Elimelech and his sons die leaving no seed or future inheritance, but Ruth marries Boaz bringing them back into the lineage of Elimelech. In the same way that Elimelech's decision had a domino affect of despair for years to come, Naomi's decision restored promise and hope to the multiple generations of her family that followed.

Miracle: Instead of removing the family heritage, Naomi's decision to return and Ruth's decision to follow not only reinstated them into a genealogy of inheritance, but into the Messianic lineage. The actual bloodline from which Jesus Christ Himself would come years later.

Miracle: Ruth, whose name means 'companion-friend', married their kinsman/redeemer Boaz and became the mother of their first child Obed, whose name means 'formed worshiper'. Obed then had a son named Jesse, which means 'to exist, to stand out'. Jesse then had a son named David, meaning 'beloved-friend'. The birth of Obed, formed worshiper, was a celebration of praise unto God for His great mercy. What a wonderful reminder that God restored them into Israel's heritage.

Obed must have grown up hearing the stories of God's redemption. He saw the example of his grandmother Naomi and his mother Ruth and how they followed after God. Not much is actually said about Obed, but the testimony of his decision is evident in his grandson, David's life. The 'formed worshiper', must have spent a lot of time in the fields with his grandson, David, mentoring him as we see years later David is known as the "Worshiper of God".

Could it be that when David was worshiping in the temple with the other psalmists he was reflecting on times he and his grandfather, the formed worshiper, would play the harp and worship God while keeping his father's sheep in the fields? Could it be that by humbling himself before God in worship he learned how to be a servant so God could trust him with the office of king? I believe that Obed's example influenced David's heart of worship giving him the title as "a man after God's own heart!" (1 Samuel 13:14)

This is the power of God's restoration! He took Elimelech's failures and revealed His great power to restore. Elimelech had forgotten the 'God of all authority, the Supreme Ruler', he left the land of God's Provision, losing everything in search of 'Man's Solution'. Yet God restored all and more to his lineage through the decision of his widow, Naomi, to return to the Land of Promise and her widowed Moabite daughter-in-law, Ruth, who chose to follow as her 'companion-friend'.

Your influence does matter! The generational blessings as well as curses attest to this throughout the ages. Your decisions can change the destiny of generations to come. One decision almost took Elimelech's family completely 'out' of the blessing. Yet one decision secured their position 'in' the blessing. Only one decision, just one!

"Your decisions can change the destiny of generations to come."

Don't flippantly make decisions. Once a decision is made, it begins affecting people faster than we can calculate, and don't even begin to think that you can fix it. God is the only one who is able to intervene. Once you decide to walk outside of the place of God's Provision by not aligning yourself with His Word, by gossiping, backbiting, engaging in ungodly behavior, or by justifying your marginal 'liberties', it will begin to affect the people around you.

Right now there are people in your city that hate people in your church and don't even know why? These people say things like, "Oh I don't go to church because of this person or that person." Then come to find out they don't even know the person they're talking about. They actually know the person, who was told by the person, who was told by someone else who knows the person.

The saddest part about it all is that many times the original 'someone' who started the whole rumor was actually a part of your church and began 'speaking' when he or she should have drank a tall glass of 'shut-up' and went back to prayer. But instead, ten years later an innocent bystander who needs Jesus won't come to church and probably won't even be open to receiving the gospel of Jesus Christ all because of one person's misguided influence.

Of course what that individual doesn't realize is that the original two people who had the disagreement actually patched things up and were friends again in less than a week. But that poor person is still out there stuck in a shell somewhere because one decision made by one person to speak ill of someone else. All because of one person's decision to seek justice for self rather than to let God do the justification.

One decision, just one! Your one decision can affect the lives of multiple people, even hundreds of thousands of people over the course of your life.

So what decisions are you making? Will you decide today that you will no longer allow yourself to be motivated by circumstance, but be motivated instead by a necessity to honor and glorify God?

Do you posses the Fear of God? Or is He just your Buddy? Do you truly love Him? Or is He just your boyfriend? Jesus said, "If you love me keep My commandments" (John 14:15). Maybe you're just content with Him loving you. Does He exist to meet your needs and respond to your beckon call? Or do you exist for His pleasure? Are you willing to die to your agenda and leave Man's Solutions behind?

Will you decide to pursue God and allow his Provision to escort you into His Promise and become the place you choose to live?

Will you decide to be accountable enough to realize that others are following your lead and be responsible for the actions that you show them?

Will you decide to give life and hope to those around you by teaching through your life and your words the glorious gospel of Christ and the commandments of God?

Will you stop relying on the church to bring your children to Christ and start raising them in the Word of God yourself?

Will you be the one to start leading them into the roles of a Godly man and woman by your own example and instruction?

Will you re-establish yourself as the bride of Christ and live your life according to his Word?

Will you be willing to travail for the lost and dying of this world that you might birth spiritual babies into the kingdom and disciple them into servants and worshipers of God?

Will you make the decision to affect your generation and the generations to come by living a positive Godly example today, tomorrow and for the rest of your life?

Will you take the chance and make the decision that will reinstate your name into the line of His inheritance and break the curses provoked by decisions made by you and the generations that went before you?

Well, will you? Will YOU?! If so then WHEN?

You might have made just one decision that you aren't sure if God can ever correct. But I assure you that today, if you decide to fully follow Christ, God will begin to take what has spanned over years of destruction at your hand and in a moment begin to start the correcting process that will restore to you what the years have stolen away.

Beginning today you will have the opportunity to speak into the hearts and lives of people about the goodness of

God. Make the decision to have a thankful heart toward the One True God for His miraculous provision and care. Decide to take the narrow less traveled path and make a difference in the lives of those around you, proving that God rules and reigns in the hearts of those who decide to follow Him, or will you choose the wide and well traveled road and succumb to the past.

What decision will you make? Choose today to be a Heritage maker and a Lineage changer. Prepare your heart to pour out your life as an offering, a sweet smelling sacrifice unto God, choose to be thankful. Thankful that we serve a God that can reverse the effects of our fallen humanity, redeem us back to Himself and save us from the 'impact of our decisions'! (See Romans 8:28)

"Choose today to be a Heritage maker and a Lineage changer."

I Corinthians 15:20-22:

> *"But now is Christ risen from the dead, and become the first fruits of them that slept. For since by man came death, by man came also the resurrection of the dead. For as in Adam all die, even so in Christ shall all be made alive."*

Three very simple scriptures, yet within them lay a life transforming reality. Do yourself a favor and write these on several post-it-notes and stick them everywhere you will see them.

The scripture in Corinthians tells us that Christ rose from the dead and became the first fruits of them that had previously died prior to Christ's redemptive work. Regardless of how good they were in life, they could not enter into God's presence because of the original sin that plagued humanity.

This is obviously a difficult concept for us to understand. Jesus, all God, and all man, all at once. Somehow, beyond our understanding, God fused Himself with His original sinless creation to become both the Son of God and the son of man in one person, Jesus Christ. He came to earth to fulfill His covenant and reconcile us to Himself. He paid the debt of our sin by taking our penalty upon Himself.

One mistake we often make is pretending that we understand the complexities of redemption, when in reality many times we are left scratching our head in a state of wonder. I have come to realize I will never fully understand the miracles of God, yet I have chosen to rest in the confidence that His love for me is enough.

Look at a flower, or pick up one blade of grass and we see the majesty of His creation, the awe of His miraculous power. God reveals Himself to us in portions, in pieces, mysteries of heaven that are revealed only through His Holy Spirit.

While on the isle of Patmos, Apostle John received the most dynamic insight into the end times that man has ever known, a direct download from the Holy Spirit that came with a guided tour by a heavenly host. Even as John penned the last words of the Book of Revelation I believe he returned to his bed overwhelmed with the meaning of it all.

"Yes, He loved me that much."

There is one thing of which I am certain. I know that God the Father was so intent on restoring our fellowship with Him that He sent His only begotten Son, Jesus Christ, to insure each of us the opportunity to re-establish a communion with Him and save me from my sins and an eternity separated from Him. Yes, He loved me that much.

Somehow, through the miraculous power and redemptive work that was completed through Jesus' sacrifice, I have been brought back into a right standing with God. Because I have repented of my sin against God and made the decision to trust in Christ's completed redemption for me, when this life is over, I will be able to enter into the throne room of heaven and for eternity be with the Father.

Paul goes on to tell us that by man came death, in Adam all have died. Wow! What a thing to have looming over your head. Every time somebody calls out your name, "Hey Adam, dinner is ready.", they are reminded that everybody died because of you. In society today, we dilute the strength and power of things because we cannot handle the truth. We're so worried about offending someone that we withhold that which could change their life.

We even begin to justify Adam's disobedience as, "Well he was just the first guy to make a mistake." Yes, I will agree that it could have been any one of us if we were the first human on the planet, but the point is that Adam doesn't need, nor do I believe he wants, anyone standing up for him. Believe me, he knows what he did and he lived with it until the day he died at 930 years old.

Regardless of who it was, we must understand the reality of what happened when Adam rebelled against God's command. Upon his willful act of disobedience, Adam sold all of humanity into slavery to sin. We have lived with this curse ever since that time. But just as through Adam came death, through Jesus Christ came life.

"But in Christ all will live."

We need to understand that Adam actually 'walked' with God. Every day God walked with Adam through the garden. Adam was filled with questions, and God was ready to provide the answers. Maybe He would share the mysteries of heaven and the miracle of creation. Adam's mind would be illuminated and inspired with perfect knowledge and understanding. But something happened, Adam sinned. In Adam all died, but in Christ all will live.

Through Christ all, not a preselected few, but all have the opportunity to be made alive or as scripture puts it "quickened". Ephesians 2:1-5 says,

> *And you hath he **quickened**, who were dead in trespasses and sins; Wherein in time past ye walked according to the course of this world, according to the prince of the power of the air, the spirit that now worketh in the children of disobedience: Among whom also we all had our conversation in times past in the lusts of our flesh, fulfilling the desires of the flesh and of the mind; and were by nature the children of wrath, even as others. But God, who is rich in mercy, for his great love wherewith he loved us, Even when we were dead in sins, hath **quickened** us together with Christ, (by grace ye are saved;)*

God has given us some incredible insight on the book of Ruth. Let's summarize a little about what we've learned and tie it into the bigger picture of the story. Let's take a look at the parallels of redemption we have observed and its comparison with the Gospel message. In four small chapters, among 66 books, God explains His entire plan to redeem His creation from beginning to end.

In Christianity, many times we see CHRIST-mas, the baby Jesus, with all the gifts and festivities, and we think the Gospel story started there, when in fact it did not start there at all. We have to go back to the beginning. Back to a man that walked with God, a man that was so personal with God, and so intimate that it goes beyond our comprehension. We have to find the similarities between the beginning of the story and compare it to the story of Ruth. The similarities between the decisions of two men, Adam and Elimelech, and the effects that followed.

Both Adam and Elimelech made terrible decisions to follow the desire of their flesh rather than the counsel of God. Their desires were birthed out of the need to care for the feelings of the flesh. Similarly they made the decision to leave the land of God's provision, to go to the land of man's solution.

Adam was faced with circumstance in the midst of a beautiful garden, having an absolutely beautiful wife, living in an absolutely perfect world. In the midst of God's blessing, yet he allowed a lust for more than God's provision to drive him into making a decision that sold out the entire human race.

"If it wasn't for a woman…"

Elimelech followed the pattern of his forefather Adam and allowed himself to be motivated by circumstance and emotion rather than follow the counsel of God. It's not about the fact that Adam followed the counsel of his wife. It is a little comic relief to me when I hear individuals blame Eve for the fall of mankind. "If it wasn't for a woman..." they ramble on. Scripture tells us in 1 Timothy 2:13-14 that the woman was the one who was deceived. So what does this tell us about Adam? Adam was, in fact, the one to whom God had give the original commandment regarding the tree. Adam had been given the responsibility to protect his wife and the authority to correct his wife's deception. In Numbers 30:6-8, Scripture tells us that the husband has the authority to cancel or retract a vow made by his wife if he acts immediately upon hearing it.

So the weight of the fall does NOT lie on Eve, but rather on Adam. Adam could have canceled the transaction of events if he would have acted immediately. But he chose to follow and fulfill the desires and lusts of his flesh rather than adhere to the counsel of God. In so doing, his decision removed him from the land of God's Provision and exiled him, his wife and the entire human race to the land of man's solution.

The decision was made in an instant, but the process that led up to his decision took time. It is highly probable that he allowed himself to be drawn away by the demands of his responsibilities and the relationship he was developing with his new wife and failed to continue spending time with his Creator. Eve was deceived, but Adam fell headlong. He was the one that actually heard the word from the Lord. Immediately upon making the decision to break God's commandment, the spiritual connection between God and man was broken.

Adam knew something had went very wrong. He was used to being in daily communion with God, walking and talking with Him in the cool of the day. He may not have been quite sure what it was he was feeling for the first time, but he knew in his heart that it wasn't good. Adam found out firsthand what it felt like to be separated from his Maker, a feeling that would haunt humanity from that moment on. Shortly after this, God calls them to Himself to inquire of the incident to which they hesitantly confess, but not before attempting to point the finger of blame away from themselves and ultimately placing it on God.

Counter to popular belief, God established order and authority beginning with the family unit. In Genesis chapter 3, God opens His questioning not with Eve, not with the serpent, but with Adam. Sadly enough, Adam shows no remorse or offers no repentance. Instead he begins by blaming Eve, who in-turn follows Adam's lead and points blame to the serpent.

Upon closer inspection you will find that in fact Adam and Eve were both blaming God for this shortcoming. Adam initially blamed Eve then added, "The woman whom thou gavest to be with me", then Eve blames the serpent, whom God created and placed in the garden, for "deceiving me".

"What if...?"

Not once during this brief discourse do we see any attempt at repentance from Adam or Eve. I can only wonder what would have happened if Adam would have immediately interceded for his wife. Scripture tells us that Adam was "with" her (Gen 3:6) when this event took place. What if Adam, before Eve even had the chance to be deceived, would have grabbed the serpent by the neck and went directly to God with a report of the serpent's attempt to sabotage God's plan? What if Adam and Eve would have made the decision to follow God's instructions regardless of whether or not they had a perfect understanding of its purpose?

Adam died spiritually that day, and the entire human race with him. Elimelech also died when he chose the land of man's solution over the Land of God's Provision. Regardless who you are or where you've been, when you make the choice to dwell in the land of man's solution, you too will die. But God didn't leave us exiled to the land of man's solution, the day He pronounced judgement on Adam and Eve, He also gave hope in the promise of a redeemer (Gen 3:15). A redeemer that would come from the seed of the woman and although the serpent would bruise the heal of the Child, the Child would crush the head of the serpent.

As Adam looked out on the growing human race and their fallen state, he must have felt hopeless of ever seeing a future redemption from the effects of his decision.

Naomi must have had the same feeling as she looked upon the effects of her dead husband's decision. It seemed that death was eminent and her family would be completely cut out of the lineage of Israel. But Naomi was motivated by necessity. All she knew was that she had to return to the land of God's provision, it's all she had. Not knowing if she would be welcomed or what would await her, only knowing that it is there that God's promises were established for His people.

God instituted the Law to redirect a fallen mankind back to a right standing with God and return them to the land of God's Provision. The Law was to be a guide to assist the human race in coming back to God. In a parallel, Naomi represents the Law. She also was a guide to Ruth.

Naomi had a driving desire to return to the place where she knew God would be. The place where one day in the distant future the people of Israel would encounter their Redeemer. But the Law in itself offers little hope. The Law continues to push on just as Naomi pushed forward on her journey, yet having no redemptive power to restore what had been lost.

"She made the decision to forsake all..."

Without the assurance of restoration, Naomi developed a hatred of her life. At one point she renamed herself Mara, meaning bitter. In the same way humanity can become bitter with life, feeling that death is imminent and in the Law alone there is no restoration.

Then Ruth is introduced into the bleak scenario of Naomi's situation. Ruth may be seen as a representation of mankind, a resident native of the land of Moab, the land of man's solution. Ruth becomes discontent with her state of life, just as the human race becomes discontented with their fallen state. Ruth was tired of what she had and longed for more. She made the decision to forsake all and follow her mother-in-law as she pursued the God of Israel.

Ruth embraced Naomi as her own mother. Although Naomi could not of herself give her a new life, she would be the one to lead her in hopes of such a life. In the same way humanity is to embrace the Law, although it has no power to redeem us within itself, it is an inspiring hope for a future that will restore us to a right standing with God.

Let's be honest with ourselves, the only reason we love God is because he loved us first (1 John 4:19). We despised even our knowledge of Him yet even though we willfully practiced sin, He chose to extend His love toward us by offering His Son to cover the penalty of our sin and reconcile us back to Himself. Do we really appreciate what He did for us? I mean really?

"But God…"

If we had a clear picture of the sacrifice He made for us, wouldn't you think our behaviors would surely reflect that? Understanding that He rescued us from our exiled fallen state and paid the debt that we could have never paid, we should be willing to forsake everything to follow Him. Through its various rituals and sacrifices, the Law led us to an understanding of God's Holiness and what is required to stand in His presence. The Law identified us as those unworthy of approaching God because of our sin.

But God had a plan. The Law drew us out from the land of man's solution and returned us to the Land of God's Provision. God was waiting just inside the entrance of the city. He was longing for the day that we would return to His Land of Provision. At the entrance was a cross shaped door that hindered us from reaching God. Hanging on this cross was the image of what appeared to be a man stretched across its beams. This man was so badly beaten he was barely recognizable as human.

We desperately want to reach God, yet it's obvious there is only one way to Him which is through the reproachful symbol of the cross and the sacrifice that was hanging from it.

Upon closer examination, we realize that this twisted malformed figure is in fact the ransom for our soul. This wasn't just any man, this was the Son of God. Perfect, Holy and innocent before God, yet He offered Himself up as we would never have been able to. At that moment, we realize why we have returned and who it was we were standing in front of. This Savior actually saw me in my state of exile and filth and took upon Himself that which we could no longer carry. This is my Redeemer! He restored life to me by forgiving me of my sin and redeeming me back to my Creator. I trust in Him for He is worthy!

God's desire is for us to repent of our sin and trust in the completed work of His Son to stand in as our Redeemer and restore us to a right relationship. God longs to be intimately connected with us as one and to give us divine purpose.

As I was then welcomed into the Land of God's Provision, I found myself enveloped by the arms of God feeling the intimacy that I had so longed for. Looking back at the cross I no longer saw the twisted form, instead my eyes gazed upon Him who was seated at the right hand of the Most High God. It was Him, Jesus Christ and I now know that my Redeemer lives!

Isn't it interesting that Ruth and Naomi went back to Bethlehem? Is it a coincidence that Boaz, the redeemer for Ruth and Naomi came from Bethlehem? Is it a coincidence that the Redeemer of mankind came out of Bethlehem? There are no coincidences in God's work. He is revealing to you the greatness of His power, the depths of His love, and the greatness of His Divine Providence.

CHAPTER 11
LIVING IN REDEMPTION

When Naomi saw the hope of their redemption, she embraced Ruth and gave her instruction. Approach him with humility, because we have nothing to offer him. He is our only hope, our only chance. In the same way, the Law took mankind and embraced it and said, "Look, there is your Redeemer. The One I have been leading you to all this time."

We should fall on our faces humbly before God at the feet of Jesus. When Jesus stirs, and he turns to gaze upon us we should say, "Please throw your covering over me. Cover me with Your authority. I need Your forgiveness. I need your protection. I need your love. I need your care. Oh redeem me, please! I am a stranger in this land. I have nothing and I am nothing. I am destitute. I cannot make it without you!"

We talk about repentance. We witness people who pray to God asking for forgiveness. Yet something must have gone very wrong, I don't understand. They aren't different. They aren't changed. They are still continuing to do the same things they used to do. Go to the same places, they used to go. Their language is the same. Their lifestyle is the same. They're exactly the same person they were asking God to forgive them for being. What happened? Could it be that they really didn't see the point of their destruction? Could it be that they really didn't see their point of need? Did they only go through this as a ceremony and really never fall before the feet of their Redeemer and plead with Him to cover them with His mercy?

"Humility is the key to breaking generational curses..."

There is one thing that will keep the sin of our generation and the generations of our forefathers continuing into the generations of our children, denial. The root of denial is pride. When we fail to confess our faults and failures and admit that we have needlessly and even intentionally hurt and offended our fellow man, that we have sinned in the sight of God in every area of our life, you can guarantee it will happen again.

When we refuse to admit to our wife how we may have failed as a husband, or to our husband that we may have failed as a wife. When we refuse to admit to our children our failures as parents, our failures in our finances, our failures in our relationships. When we refuse to look those things straight in the eye and confront them in a spirit of humble repentance, we will undoubtedly continue those cycles with a vengeance in generations to come and the blame will fall on your lap at the Great White Thrown Judgment when the secrets of your heart will be revealed for all to see.

Humility is the key to breaking generational curses from the past as well as the present.

We must humble ourselves before God. We must truly realize the state of depravity that we are in. We must truly realize that without God we were going to Hell. We were nothing, we had nothing, and everything we did was of no value to the Kingdom of God. Regardless of how good it might have seemed if it was not done under the covering of our Redeemer, it was nothing. At the very moment when Boaz heard Ruth's request, he saw a humble woman who was petitioning on behalf of her mother-in-law. He heard the cry of one who openly admitted her inadequacy and her plea for redemption.

It was then, at that moment, with the same conviction that Elimelech made the decision to move his family into the land of man's solution, that Boaz made the decision to redeem them back into the Land of God's Provision. Even though Ruth had not yet seen it, in the mind of Boaz the redemption was already complete.

It is the same way in the spirit. When we cry in a humble desperation, openly admitting our inadequacy and acknowledging our dependence upon Him, Christ looks on you with open arms and says, "It's already done. You are redeemed."

When Boaz gave Ruth six measures of barley to take to Naomi as an interest on a covenant that he promised to keep, Naomi didn't just see six measures of barley, she saw a lifetime of redemption. She saw barns full of grain. She saw their life prosperous again. She saw them reintegrated back into the lineage of Israel. She saw them reinstated into a right standing with their homeland. She was home, back in the Land of God's Provision.

Since Boaz is only a type and shadow of the true Redeemer it comes as no surprise that Jesus followed the same pattern that He laid out for Boaz to follow so many years earlier. The Bible says that we are sealed with the Spirit of Promise, which is our earnest (interest payment) from God. This interest payment is the Holy Spirit. Jesus told His disciples that He was sending the Holy Spirit to let them know that His word is good, His promise is true and their redemption is secure.

Of course you probably know what interest is. Interest is only a small portion, a fraction of an entire purchased product given in advance as a security for a pledge. Wow! If the portion of the Holy Spirit we have received is just an interest payment, only a small portion of what God has for us, what awaits us on the other side? What will the fullness of our redemption bring? What majesty will we behold? It will go beyond our understanding, beyond our comprehension.

There is an interesting point to this, which is that the redemption is not over. I know that the fulness of my redemption is still incomplete. I realize that in the Spirit it is done, complete, but throughout the Bible, God tells us that the things we see on this planet are only types and shadows of what is existing in the spirit realm. Because of this all creation is awaiting the fullness of its redemption (Romans 8:18-27).

The complete manifestation has not happened yet. The proof that we are still waiting for its fulness is all around us. The earth is still producing thistles and thorns. Part of the curse was that man would have to fight the enemies of the soil, he would have to till the ground with the sweat of his brow in order to force things to grow instead of it growing naturally as it was designed.

Another proof of the fact that we are still waiting on the fulness of our redemption is the fact that everybody still needs to wear clothes. Yes, believe me some more than others. Why is that? We are still wearing clothes because regardless of what varied cultures tell us, it is a shame to be naked.

I love what Matthew Henry, a minister from the 17th century, said in his commentary in summary, "We try to imagine a certain way we want to look and then spend a lot of money on threads that are sewn together in various patterns to form clothes." "Clothes," he goes on to say, "… disgust me. They are nothing more than a badge of shame. A reminder of my fallen state and my reason to cryout for the completion of my redemption."

If you have repented of your sin against God and trusted in Jesus for your salvation, then you are His child and as members of Christ's Body, we are clothed in His Righteousness. Stay strong in the Lord, be not weary in well doing for in due season ye shall reap a reward if you faint not. Jesus Christ is coming back and when our redemption is fulfilled, we shall become His bride. We are to take this time to ready ourselves for His soon coming. We must be working in the harvest fields of our Redeemer? Are our hearts ready? Will we be found by Him to be pure and holy, a bride that is without spot or wrinkle? A bride that is ready to welcome the King of kings and Lord of lords?

"The fulfillment of redemption is a process."

God has given us a small glimpse in just four short chapters of the entire Bible. In one tiny book in the midst of sixty-six books, He has outlined for us the entire plan of redemption from beginning to end. If we truly understand the reality of redemption, we will not be as likely to take it for granted. The fulfillment of redemption is a process. Elimelech made a decision to turn away from God and to take his family to the land of man's solution.

As we have seen it took several years and much personal loss for his family to return to the Land of God's Provision. Adam too made the decision to turn from God's Word, leaving behind His Provision and being exiled to the land of man's solution. From that day on, God has been orchestrating His plan to redeem the world back to Himself.

The pain, the suffering, the trials and tribulations. It was never supposed to be like this. We were supposed to be walking with God in the garden. We were supposed to be co-creating and co-laboring with Him. All of this because of one decision, just one. But God made a decision that would trump those made prior and once our redemption is fulfilled, the bride will be joined with the Bridegroom.

Ruth and Boaz brought forth a son named Obed, servant-worshiper. As the bride of Christ we need to be doing the same, giving birth to servant-worshipers. If we are true worshipers of God, if we truly understand the greatness of His mercy and grace toward us, we will dedicate ourselves to birthing, raising up and discipling servant worshippers that have His heart and will fulfill His commission. This would be a sight we have not experienced in its fulness. These are those who will fill the courts of Heaven when time is no more and eternity abides.

If you are not a servant, start serving. If you are not a worshiper, start worshiping. There are no job applications for anything else in Heaven. Everything we do in Christ's name and for His glory must be birthed out of the heart of the servant worshiper. The servant worshipers will resound throughout all eternity singing the high praises of our God. We have the privilege of being a part of that right now. We don't have to wait until we enter Heaven's ranks, we can start today!

The glorious completion of the redemption that we await is revealed in Revelation 5:1-3:

> *"And I saw in the right hand of him that sat on the throne a book written within and on the backside, sealed with seven seals. And I saw a strong angel proclaiming with a loud voice, Who is worthy to open the book, and to loose the seals thereof? And no man in heaven, nor in earth, neither under the earth, was able to open the book, neither to look thereon. And I wept much, because no man was found worthy to open and to read the book, neither to look thereon."*

At one point there were in fact tears and even weeping from Heaven's inhabitants. There was no redeemer to be found. No one to save dying humanity. This was definitely a time for crying, Revelation 5:5-14.

> *"And one of the elders saith unto me, Weep not: behold, the Lion of the tribe of Judah, the Root of David, hath prevailed to open the book, and to loose the seven seals thereof. And I beheld, and lo, in the midst of the throne and of the four beasts, and in the midst of the elders, stood a Lamb as it had been slain, having seven horns and seven eyes, which are the seven Spirits of God sent forth into all the earth.*

And he came and took the book out of the right hand of him that sat upon the throne. And when he had taken the book, the four beast and four and twenty elders fell down before the Lamb, having every one of them harps, and golden vials full of odors, which are the prayers of the saints. And they sung a new song, saying, Thou art worthy to take the book, and to open the seals thereof: for thou wast slain, and hast redeemed us to God by thy blood out of every kindred, and tongue, and people, and nation; And hast made us unto our God kings and priests: and we shall reign on the earth. And I beheld, and I heard the voice of many angels round about the throne and the beasts and the elders: and the number of them was ten thousand, and thousand, and thousands of thousands; Saying with a loud voice, Worthy is the Lamb that was slain to receive power, and riches, and wisdom, and strength, and honor, and glory, and blessing. And every creature which is in heaven, and on the earth, and under the earth, and such as are in the sea, and all that are in them, heard I saying, Blessing, and honor, and glory, and power, be unto him that sitteth upon the throne, and unto the Lamb for ever and ever. And the four beasts said, Amen. And the four and twenty elders fell down and worshiped him that liveth for ever and ever."

All of creation was rejoicing because the Redeemer has come and the manifestation of His work is now complete. The plan of a redemption had to be set in place all because of one man's decision. But God in his ultimate overwhelming, incomprehensible grace, mercy, and love, has provided that redemption for us if we will just repent and trust in His Son Jesus Christ.

We no longer have to live under the cloud of failure or of hopelessness. Because of our Redeemer we can live in peace with God, in victory over death, hell and the grave. We can live free of fear and torment in anticipation of the hope of our full and complete redemption. In addition, He has given us His Holy Spirit as partial payment to comfort, guide and empower us for the fulfillment of our assignment, to bring this glorious Gospel message to the world while there is still time.

"Behold, your redeemer has come!"

Neither CHRIST-mas nor Easter are to be considered the beginning or even the end. They are only reflections of two of the most recognizable signs of God's manifested process of our redemption.

That same redemptive process that has been moving ahead since the fall of man and will continue until the completion of time. The redemption of mankind has been completed in the spirit but its final victory must be played out in the earth. Romans 8:19 says:

"For the earnest expectation of the creature waiteth for the manifestation of the sons of God."

Luke 2:6 continues:

"And so it was while they were there, the days were accomplished that she should be delivered. She brought forth her first-born son, And wrapped Him in swaddling clothes and laid Him in a manger; because there was no room for them

in the inn. And there were in the same country shepherds abiding in the field keeping watch over their flock by night. And lo the angel of the Lord came upon them and the glory of the Lord shown round about them and they were sore afraid and the angels said unto them, 'Fear not. For, behold, I bring you good tidings of great joy which shall be to all people. For unto you is born this day in the city of David a Saviour, which is Christ the Lord."

The One who was of the lineage of Ruth and of David approximately 1200 years after Ruth's death. The son of the living God, the Savior, the Messiah, Jesus Christ the Lord, behold, your Redeemer has come!

The Story of Ruth is an incredible revealing of our redemptive value in the hands of the One, True God. It's a story of His love for us as His creation and how He reconciled us back to Himself even in our most valiant efforts to thwart Him.

CHAPTER 12
IT ONLY TAKES ONE

In chapter one, I shared with you about the time I made the decision not to follow what I felt God was leading me to do. Instead I accepted the offer of more money and promotion, all in the name of taking care of my family. In the heat of the moment I lost focus on God's provision and stepped into my solution. So here's how that story ended.

About one week after being told our crew wouldn't be on the road for at least a few months we were called out to a project that would keep me on the road and away from home for the next four months.

Leaving my very pregnant wife alone in our little rental house in the small town of Oro Grande, California, was unnerving to say the least, but I had agreed to return to the crew so off I went. Oh, did I mention we had no home phone?

Our three-man crew was only on the road for about two weeks when we were called out to a night job which required some intense wielding of ten pound wrenches and twenty pound sledge hammers, all while straddling various pipe configurations and open ditches. Everything was fine until the next morning, I could barely move. After a trip to the doctor I was told a muscle in my back had been over-stretched and recovery would require three solid weeks on my back in bed. Ahhhhhh! What?! Are you kidding me?!?!

God has such a sense of humor, and just to make sure I didn't cheat at all you'll never believe what happened next. At the ripe old of age of twenty-one, while laying on my back in bed, I contracted Chicken Pox. Yep, I never had them as a child so now was the time. Not only was I bound to the bed, but now I was quarantined to the bedroom! For the next three to four weeks my beautiful pregnant wife nursed me back to health with all the love I could have ever wanted.

Now here's the kicker, the same week I injured myself our crew was notified that the four month project we were assigned to had been postponed to a later date so they returned home.

I ended up never returning to my crew. I chose to leave the land of my solution, and instead I returned to the Land of God's Provision. God has never left me and it was through this experience I learned to trust His Divine Providence to lead me each step of the way ever since.

"Choose wisely, time is short."

Decisions. It only takes one. One decision to exile you to the land of man's solution. One decision to return you to the Land of God's Provision.

Choose wisely, time is short.

Author Robert D. Kee is an interpersonal communication specialist, motivational speaker, generational leadership trainer, and life strategist. He has spent his life in the pursuit of equipping others to connect with their prospective audiences effectively through efficient communication and conversational intelligence. He has spent a quarter of a century using his expertise in corporate as well as nonprofit spheres, working with both teams and individuals.

Kee has been married to Belinda for thirty-four years, and together they have a daughter, a son and a daughter-in-law, and three beautiful grandchildren.